HISTORY & GUIDE

Plymouth

HISTORY & GUIDE

Plymouth

JOHN VAN DER KISTE

Frontispiece: The Barbican. *Above:* A post-war greeting from Plymouth. (Both courtesy of M. Richards)

First published 2009

The History Press
The Mill, Brimscombe Port
Stroud, Gloucestershire, GL5 2QG
www.thehistorypress.co.uk

British Library Cataloguing in Publication Data.
A catalogue record for this book is available from the British Library.

ISBN 978 0 7509 5122 7

Typesetting and origination by The History Press
Printed in Great Britain

Contents

Also by John Van der Kiste

Foreword and Acknowledgements

Over the last 150 years, several others have written and published their own histories of Plymouth. The tradition, from Llewellynn Jewitt and R.N. Worth in the Victorian era, to Crispin Gill and John Gerrard in the closing years of the twentieth century, is an honourable one. As another, R.A.J. Walling, writing shortly after the Second World War, noted in his closing paragraphs, the story of Plymouth 'can but end raggedly.' In adding the present volume to what is already available I might plead a similar ragged end while the city is in the throes of another major transformation.

From prehistoric times to the present day, Plymouth has undergone numerous changes. A visitor coming to the city after the post-Second World War reconstruction programme was completed in the 1960s would have found a very different sight to that seen by someone a century earlier. In the first decade of the twenty-first century, the city is once again in the throes of further development which will see it transformed to meet the demands and challenges of a modern age, making much of it unrecognisable to those who were familiar with the Plymouth of forty or fifty years earlier.

I have therefore endeavoured to tell the story from prehistoric times to its status on the threshold of a new age, from its position as a thriving centre of commerce in medieval times dependent on the sea, to that of one of the leading defence establishments in times of war, and to the present-day situation after the Cold War which sees it no longer reliant on the armed services as it was for so many years.

Though not a Plymothian born or bred, I can lay some claim to belonging to the city, having worked there almost continuously in public and academic libraries since leaving school. My father, Wing Commander R.E.G. Van der Kiste, served with the Royal Auxiliary Air Force at Mount Batten and was later secretary, then director, of the Plymouth Chamber of Trade and Commerce for many years. I am proud and pleased to have had an opportunity to write the present volume, and I know he and my mother would have taken pride and interest in the project as well.

Particular thanks are due to my wife Kim, for her constant encouragement, interest, and indefatigable photography of Plymouth as the occasion demanded, and to Hannah and James, who helped her in reading the final manuscript; to my Plymouth-born editor Matilda Richards, for originally commissioning the work (appropriately, over lunch in a very good hostelry overlooking the city's historic Sutton Harbour) and for her constant encouragement while the work was in progress, to say nothing of seeing the book through the press; and to her assistant, Beth Amphlett. I would also like to place on record my debt to Chris Robinson, whose knowledge of, and passion for, the history of Plymouth must be second to none, and who allowed me to pick his brains from time to time; to Chris Downer, Colin McCormick, and Steve Johnson, for permission to use photographs; to Russell Parkin, for additional photography; to the staff at the Local Studies Collection, Plymouth City Libraries, for their help during my research; to John Carter, for the loan of invaluable material; and to Brian Moseley, whose website on the history of Plymouth has proved an unfailingly useful 'enquire within' service online.

John Van der Kiste, 2009

The author enjoying the view across the city's historic Sutton Harbour.

one

Prehistoric, Roman and Saxon Plymouth

From prehistoric to medieval times, much of Plymouth's history is inevitably shrouded in some mystery. Archaeological excavations made mostly during the nineteenth century have indicated ancient settlements and evidence of trading, while between the Norman Conquest and Tudor times there are also the records of chroniclers to put a little more flesh on the bare bones of basic fact. Nevertheless the archaeology of south-west England can only lead us to a certain amount of supposition, while contemporary historians' records often conflict with one another, particularly on the course of events. None of these can be regarded as totally accurate. Our knowledge of early Plymouth, therefore, must be regarded as built partly on guesswork. One can hardly do better than quote the doyen of modern Plymouth historians, Crispin Gill, who commented on the difficulties he had in writing his 'early chapters about periods of which we have little real knowledge,' and of the temptation to speculate. As far as the early days are concerned, it is largely a matter of speculation – or silence.

The existence of Plymouth from the prehistoric era was determined by its surrounding physical geography, with the River Plym, the drowned valley of the River Tamar and its tributaries dominating the area and determining the land use between them. All the valleys were deeply cut by their rivers and subsequently drowned or inundated by the sea at the end of the last Ice Age, and the south Devon coastline reached inland along these deep river valleys, thus producing excellent deep-water anchorages. The coastline was cut into many small peninsulas, thus impeding communication by land. Numerous creeks stretched a long way inland, and had to be crossed by fords or bridges high upstream of the muddy inlets. The silting up or deliberate in-filling of many creeks in later years masked the impact that the physical geography had exerted on early settlements in this area.

It was said that around 1200 BC the legendary Brutus, a great-grandson of Aeneas of Troy, known in medieval English legend as the founder and first King of Britain, came to south Devon. When he landed at Totnes he found the countryside peopled with giants who attacked the Trojans and, after a fierce battle, the latter won. At some point inland Corin or Corineus, the warrior credited with founding Cornwall (after whom the county was named) as well as leading the Trojans, had a wrestling match with Goemagot. The latter, the sole surviving giant, stood 'twelve cubits [about 20ft] high, and [was] of such strength that with one stroke he pulled up an oak as if it had been a hazel wood,' but the victorious Corin slew his opponent by throwing him into the sea. The story comes from the ninth-century *Historia Britonum*, attributed to Nennius, and the twelfth-century *Historia Regum Britanniae* by Geoffrey of Monmouth.

A surviving fragment of the fifteenth-century castle walls, Lambhay Hill.

This wrestling match was variously said to have taken place at Totnes, Dover, or Land's End, though staunch Plymothians over the years have argued that the site was actually Lambhay, the present-day Lambhay Hill, near Plymouth Hoe.

For several hundred years the contest was commemorated in a pair of huge figures cut out in turf at the place where they allegedly fought. A sixteenth-century audit book records payment of 8*d* to a Mr John Lucas for cutting out the double figure of Goemagot or Gogmagog, as it was sometimes known, and it had to be renewed by local craftsmen at regular intervals. This area of turf was destroyed when the Citadel was erected in the seventeenth century.

Such is the stuff of legend. However, C.W. Bracken has suggested that there may be some truth in the tale, and that Geoffrey was doing no more than writing down 'an embellished account of the movements of some early invading race.'

Archaeological excavations since the early nineteenth century have produced evidence of continued occupation of the Plymouth area since the Ice Age. Such discoveries include a flint arrow head found on the Hoe, and a deer-horn pick discovered in the course of excavations for Keyham Docks. The earliest known settlement in Plymouth was thought to date back to around 1000 BC with a small Iron-Age trading port located at Mount Batten near Turnchapel, where a workman found five gold and eight silver coins in the angle of a rock in or around 1832. The gold coins had been made by the Dubonni tribe of Gloucestershire and Somerset, the earliest dating back to around 125 BC, and the others were identified as having been struck in the first centuries BC or AD. An Iron-Age cemetery – exposed in 1864 between Fort Stamford and Mount Batten, during construction of the forts remembered to posterity as the 'Palmerston follies' – revealed the burial of many items in bronze, iron, earthenware and glass, as well as parts of three bronze mirrors decorated on the back with Celtic designs.

During the building of the Royal Air Force station at Mount Batten between 1917 and 1920, further discoveries included a sickle, chisel, gouges and a knife from the late

Bronze Age, and Iron-Age brooches, pins and parts of bracelets, jewellery and broken pottery thought to date from a later age, as well as Roman coins from the reigns of all or most Emperors from Nero (54–68 AD) to Gratian (367–383 AD).

Flint nodules were discovered at Cattedown, while kistvaens (prehistoric stone coffins, or small rectangular pits covered with earth and surrounded by small stones) and urns were found in the areas now occupied by Union Street and Stillman Street. All these discoveries pointed to the existence of a trading settlement occupied, perhaps continuously, from between around 800 and 1000 BC to the end of the Roman era. The site had various natural advantages, with Plymouth Sound providing shelter for the narrow entrance to the River Plym, a natural anchorage off a firm shelving beach on which boats could be run ashore, level ground behind the beach for a settlement, a narrow neck of land to the mainland, and a steep hill at the tip of the narrow strip of land bordered on either side by water. These would be invaluable for defence in time of war. Within a mile was the almost landlocked Hooe Lake, which provided suitable beaches for repairing ships. Here was an early British trading establishment. The nearest main outpost of the Roman Empire was Exeter, and Mount Batten may have been a major staging point or beacon station on the way.

Bronze axes, gouges, chisels, knives, daggers and sickle blades made out of copper and tin, discovered over the years, all indicated that several activities were taking place, from trading across the sea, to the cultivation of land, and also preparations for defence against any marauding forces. Items of jewellery such as rings, bracelets and brooches were also recovered. The settlement of people in this area may have been partly dependent for food on the sea as well as on meat, judging by the number of oyster, whelk and limpet shells found, in addition to the bones of deer, dogs and pigs.

A local trade in tin is believed to have existed here, brought to Plymouth from Dartmoor along the River Plym and traded with the ancient Phoenicians, several centuries before the coming of the Romans. During the Roman Empire, Plymouth presumably continued to trade in tin as well as cattle and hides, though as a commercial interest it was later overshadowed by the rise of the fishing village of Sutton. Cornish tin is thought to have been taken across the Tamar and then via Crownhill to the forts of the Plym, along the Ridgeway – believed to be part of a Roman road though built on the site of an earlier British trackway – then to Totnes, Exeter and overseas.

There was probably a small settlement in pre-Roman times at Stonehouse, the name of which was believed to have originated through the existence of a stone-built dwelling in the vicinity, and must have been constructed by the Romans, the only people who could have created such a sophisticated building. The peninsula of land known as Stonehouse may have been the site of a Roman villa, as it is thought that the first Saxon settlers called this place Stonehouse because they must have found a house or its ruins there. These remains were presumably substantial enough to give the area its name. Other names associated with the old civil registration districts owe their names to early settlements that grew up as isolated communities in the region, such as Plympton, Stoke Damerel and Devonport. The discovery of fragments of pottery bowls, jars, drinking cups and cooking pots were also thought to indicate the existence of scattered hamlets by the Tamar and the Plym.

During the era of Roman occupation, it is thought that the Romans buried their dead on the southern shore of Stonehouse Creek, at Newport Street. In 1882 an ancient burial place was found just below Stonehouse Bridge, and all the evidence pointed to this having been a Roman crematorium. Excavations for the construction of four cottages exposed a flat area paved with pebbles and slate slabs with a group of about fifteen small tombs of brick and stone in one corner, arranged in rows, almost certainly of Roman origin. Other excavations carried out around the same time suggested there was a Roman settlement at Trematon, on a small creek of the River Lynher, and a signal station near Kings Tamerton. The present-day Roman Way is thought to be based on a route made in Roman times from Plympton to Saltash, avoiding creeks and inlets. A theory exists that in Saxon times, if not before, the area which later came to be known as Plymouth was called Tamarworth or Tameoworth, interpreted as 'the island of the Tamar,' and named thus by St Indractus.

Towards the end of the seventh century the Saxons moved westwards from Wessex, making the Tamar estuary their new western frontier. In AD 705 King Geraint of Cornwall gave the bishop of the new diocese of Sherborne five hides of land, about 600 acres, at Maker. Devon was made a county before 800 and divided into hundreds, the original form of local government. Saxon government, land tenure and manorial rule were soon established and the hundreds were divided further into tythings, a hundred being a district of approximately a hundred families and a tything one of ten. Plymouth was originally in the hundred of Walkhampton, and later in the hundred of Roborough.

It was around this time that Plymouth as we know it today began to emerge in the shape of Sutton, or Sudtone, to give it its original title, the south town or 'ton,' the Saxon word for farm. In the late eighth or early ninth century the Danes landed in England, and are said to have come as far west as Devon and Cornwall. It is thought that in the mid-ninth century a Danish force landed at the mouth of the River Yealm, to be confronted by a force of Devonians who came up 'against the heathen man at Wembury, made great slaughter there and gained the victory.' The Danes returned around 877, burning anything in Devon in their path, but their luck turned when a hurricane dashed their ships against the rock at Mount Batten and over a hundred vessels foundered with all hands. There may have been subsequent Viking invasions, but no Danish remains have been identified in the area, although it is thought that some earthworks may be Danish in origin.

When Sutton changed its name from Tamarworth is unclear, but the Saxons set up numerous manors in the district, and the original settlement of Sutton grew up at the mouth of the River Plym. At this time it was probably fully inhabited, and a major resort for fishing. In the eleventh century it was bounded by the Sound on the south and by what is more or less modern Stonehouse on the west, extended north to the old Stoke Damerel Fleet, the later Deadlake, filled in during the nineteenth century to become Victoria Park, with Coxside as the eastern boundary. Encircled by the manors of Stonehouse, it covered an area of over 700 acres. Sutton Pool gave a sheltered anchorage and the first settlers set their farm a little way up the north bank of the pool near a stream, which provided them with fresh water. They would have been sheltered from the westerly winds and had gentle south-facing slopes for their fields. The original farm eventually became known as the old town, a small fishing village, on the northern shore of Sutton Pool, at the most southerly point of Walkhampton hundred. Its whereabouts can be identified to some extent by the street name of Old Town Street which led up to it. The original settlers, it is thought, sailed into Sutton Pool and set up farms on the north bank of the stream, a few hundred yards up its course. This area was sheltered from the westerly winds, with gentle south-facing slopes for fields, and a ready water supply for human needs and their cattle in the stream.

The early kings kept certain royal manors for strategic reasons. Sutton commanded the head of the Sound and the entrance to the River Plym, while the manor of King's Tamerton covered the Tamar crossing point and the area which still bears the name today, as well as present-day Lower St Budeaux, and the Bull Point waterfront round to Saltash Passage. The main farm in the vicinity was at Barne Barton, and a branch of Weston Mill Creek would have taken the tide close to it.

Three other manors, all larger and wealthier, were almost certainly the earliest sea settlements. Tamerton (as opposed to King's Tamerton) had a church at the head of the creek and probably the adjacent manor house. A stream running into the creek was the manor's southern boundary, and to the north it reached far up Tamarside and along the Tavy, close to the edge of Dartmoor. By Norman times, sixteen farms and six smallholdings had been carved out of the woods, and there were seven slaves at the manor farm. Among their duties, they had to operate the salt works on the marshes, by guiding the sea into shallow pans, wait for the sun to evaporate the water, then gather in the salt that was left.

Stoke (Saxon for 'dairy farm') had a church behind Stonehouse Creek, with the manor running north along Tamarside to Weston Mill Creek, where the Ham brook reached the estuary. Large mud flats formed at the confluence. Early maps showed them as the Ham ooze, or Ham mud (hence the name Hamoaze, for the modern Tamar estuary). Stoke Church is thought to mark the original settlement point, but at some stage the manor house moved to the north bank of Keyham Creek, thus taking the Celtic name of Keyham. The creek reached as far as Swilly (Saxon for 'hollow place'), and thus gave its name to Ford. Eggbuckland, the third manor, covered the area now known as Marsh Mills, going westwards, covering a large amount of meadowland and containing another salt works.

Other, smaller settlements around this time included Lipson, at the head of another creek of the Plym; Leigham, on the main stream of the Plym, at almost the highest point reached by the tide at Plym Bridge; Efford, at the Ebb Ford on the old east-west road; two different Mutleys; two different Whitleighs; Widey; Manadon; Weston; Burrington and Honicknowle; and St Budeaux on the Tamar, taking its name from St Budoc's Church. St Budoc was the Bishop of Dol in Brittany, and grandson of the fifth-century King of Brest. He was said to have sailed across the Channel to Plymouth, landed at Budshead or Tamerton Creek, founded a settlement and built a small church, which later gave way to a permanent stone one dedicated to him and erected shortly before the Norman Conquest in 1066. In Saxon times these manors started as clearings in the forest which gradually expanded, with land between the clearings being left as waste.

A monastery existed at Plympton in Saxon times, and according to a deed of 904 it came into possession of King Edward the Elder at around that time. The present church of Plympton St Mary was built on the ruins of the old priory.

For a long period Devon enjoyed peace and stability. The Tamar was an effective guard against the Cornish, and the occasional armies the Saxons had to mobilise against them used the easier crossings from Devon above the tidal reaches. Apart from the Cornish, the only enemies came from Scandinavia. Viking raids remained a threat, and never more so than in 997. According to the *Anglo-Saxon Chronicle*, that year a Viking force attacked much of the West Country and Wales, 'and there much evil wrought in burning and manslaughter.' After foraging around the coast, they proceeded up the mouth of the Tamar, 'went up until they camen to Liddyford, burning and slaying everything they met. Moreover, Ordulf's minister at Tavistock they burned to the

Tamerton Creek, the site of a Saxon settlement.

ground, and brought to their ships incalculable plunder.' Nevertheless the Plymouth area, being less a recognizable town or community than Exeter, was spared the destruction which befell the latter during a far more savage invasion five years later.

By the time of the Norman Conquest, Plymouth was still in effect a group of manors whose names can still be traced clearly in the city and its suburbs. The King was Lord of the Manor of Sutton, while the Saxon Alwin held Stanehouse (now Stonehouse), Modlei (Mutley) and Elforde (Efford), while Brismar held Stoches (Stoke), Saulf and Godwin the two Lipsons, and Heche Bocheland (Eggbuckland).

During the medieval era the settlement of Plympton was more important than Plymouth, as it had a river crossing which was deep enough for ships. The site of a castle and the old market charter are evidence of the town's status in medieval times. As the River Plym became silted up, and as ships found it increasingly difficult to navigate a route upstream, mariners and merchants regarded the mouth of the river as a more suitable area in which to develop a settlement.

Sometime around the eleventh century Plymouth developed as a fishing village belonging to the prior of Plympton, a prior being the head of a priory or small abbey. In the early thirteenth century the prior turned the village into a town by starting a market there. Once a market had been established in the village, merchants and craftsmen came to live and work there and it gradually developed into a town.

After the Normans arrived in England the manors passed to Norman owners, and much of what is now modern Plymouth was given to Judhel of Totnes Castle. The richest of Judhel's Plymouth manors was Eggbuckland, but he later let it to Stephen, his tenant in Compton. The King ordered the building of a castle at Plympton which he gave to Richard de Redvers, whom he created Earl of Devon, and kept control of the manors of Sutton, King's Tamerton (to distinguish it from Tamerton, which later became Tamerton Foliot) and Maker (Cornish for ruin). As a result the parish of Maker was officially in Devon until 1844, when it was transferred to Cornwall. The population of the entire area at the end of the eleventh century was probably less than 1,000.

At the time of the Domesday Book in 1086, almost two-thirds of the present area of Plymouth was under management. The rest was waste, or mudflats in the creeks and estuaries. The majority of farmland was arable, with only a small proportion of meadow and pasture. There were about 200 families living on the 15,000 acres of farmland scattered through thirty-one manors, 150 farms, and seventy-two smallholdings. The manors included about 450 acres of small woods and four larger woods, each over a mile long. Most of the waste moorland, woodland and heath between the clearings, which had been left by the creation of manors in pre-Norman times, were now technically part of the Royal Forest of Devon. 'Forest' referred to all land which was subject to the Royal Forest laws, and which prohibited assarting (the right of enclosure), hunting, and pasturing. Over a period of time the old forest developed into open moorland or woodland. In 1242 Devon was granted a charter of disafforestation, by which the Crown retained only the forests of Dartmoor and Exmoor.

The Domesday Survey records that Plympton was the wealthiest manor of the district and owned land in parts of Plymstock, Brixton and Shaugh. Pre-Domesday spellings of Plympton were Plymenton and Plimton. The Domesday Book spelling was Plintona, which had become Plympton by the thirteenth century. Plintona, it was believed by historian R.N. Worth, was derived from Pen-lyn-tun, the tun at the head of the lake, the Laira estuary. The river was thought to have taken its name from Plympton, and not vice versa, as is sometimes supposed. In time, Plymouth would supersede Sutton as the name of the settlement at the mouth of the Plym.

Plympton was the largest of the manors, covering more land than Stoke and Tamerton put together. Most of Plympton was in royal hands, but almost a third had been given to the Saxon priory at the head of tidal water. On its fringes were the smaller manors such as Beechwood, Challonsleigh, Elfordleigh, Langage, Loughtor and Hemerdon. Further down the creek were two manors called Woodford, on rich waterside farmland and worth as much together as the whole of Plymstock, including the meadows, woods, pastures, a salt works and a fishery. Merafield, or marshy field, a later place name, dated from the time when the creek was silting up and was more marsh than creek.

Plymstock, on the south bank of the Laira estuary, was owned by Tavistock Abbey. An old Dartmoor legend told the tale of Childe the Hunter, a man of Anglo-Saxon times, being caught in a snowstorm on the moor, having decided he would leave his manor of Plymstock to anyone who was prepared to give his body a Christian burial. After he died the monks of Tavistock got their hands on the body first, but men from Plymstock blocked their way to the bridge across the Tavy, so the Tavistock monks solved the problem by building a new bridge, Guile Bridge, higher up the river. Plymstock's smaller manors included Hooe (which was the most valuable), Goosewell, Staddon, and Staddiscombe, the two latter being mainly pasture land.

At the end of the eleventh century, the area which was about to become Plymouth was overwhelmingly agricultural. Yet economic needs and its coastal location would soon shape its history and give the town a very different character.

two

Medieval Plymouth

The death of King William I in 1087 led to a struggle between his sons for the duchy of Normandy, the family's most prized territorial possession. It was only resolved when one of the sons, Henry I, who had succeeded his childless brother William II on the English throne, besieged and captured Tinchebrai, Normandy, in 1106, thus vanquishing his brother Robert. One of the defenders of Tinchebrai was the Earl of Mortain, who was now sentenced to life imprisonment and forfeited all his estates. Renaldus de Valletort, whose local power base was at Trematon Castle on the Cornish side of the River Tamar, was one of the Cornish knights who had fought on Henry's side. As a reward after the victory he was granted the manor of Sutton.

The Valletorts were one of the most important families in the history of early Plymouth. They were probably adventurers, an old Norman family who had a remarkable ability for being on the winning side, starting with William of Normandy (the future William I) at the time of the Norman Conquest. Within a few years of coming to England they owned large amounts of land across south-east Cornwall and south Devon. Among these was the Augustinian priory at Plympton, a larger and older settlement than Plymouth, which stood at the head of the tidal estuary of the River Plym, when it was founded around 1121. In time the prior's power over the area would cause friction with the burgesses of the growing township of Plymouth. Plympton was developing fast, houses were built near the castle and the small township of Plympton Erle was gradually gaining in importance. The Earls of Devon had been given a market at Plympton Erle in 1194, while Sutton was still little more than a village.

The name Plym Mouth was first used in the Pipe Rolls for 1211 when a shipload of bacon was despatched to Portsmouth and another of wine to Nottingham, a trade which helped to establish the importance of Plymouth. It became a market town in 1254, when King Henry III gave a Charter to the priors of Plympton, granting a market with a fair on St John the Baptist's Day, as well as an assize (a thirteenth-century statute in English law that set standards of quality, measurement, and pricing for bakers and brewers, as such making it the first law in British history to regulate the production and sale of food), a ducking stool and pillory. At the same time he signed a grant giving Sutton its market, which took place every Thursday, and increased considerably the local influence of the growing town, with traders coming in from the countryside.

The relatively rapid growth of various settlements led to disputes between the different religious establishments on one hand, and the Valletort family and the priors of Plympton on the other. After some years of claims and counter-claims about who was Lord of the Manor, matters came to a head in 1281 when John Valletort claimed he held this position while the prior claimed he owned the 'ville' of Sutton. At an official enquiry held at Exeter that same year, when important evidence was given confirming the transfer of the manor of Sutton to the Valletort family by Henry I, and the rights conferred on it in the reign of Henry III, the judge ruled that the prior of Plympton's authority was limited to the built-up area, in other words the original Sutton, on the north shore of Sutton Pool, while the Valletorts were lords to the rest of Sutton, the as yet undeveloped land to the south, while the port belonged to the King. At around the same time Plympton was losing trade to Plymouth, mainly through the silting up of the Laira estuary, due to tinning activities on Dartmoor and increasing sediment carried by the rivers.

After King John had lost Normandy in 1204 to France, Plymouth became the main base in England for campaigns against France, and in 1295 the national fleet gathered for the first time off the shore of Plymouth. As a vassal of King Philippe II of France for Gascony, King Edward I had been ordered to appear before him, but had refused and Philip declared that the latter had thus forfeited his status as fief or vassal, thus in effect reclaiming Gascony from the English crown. Edward ordered the fleet to Guienne to demand the restoration of his rights, and the ships were assembled at Plymouth under the command of his brother Edmund, Earl of Lancaster. The King and his retinue came and stayed for several days at Plympton Priory. As the resources around Plymouth were not enough to supply the fleet with adequate provisions, orders were sent to every county in the King's realm to supply 2,000 quarters of wheat and oats, plus beef and pork, for the men who were going to take part in the Gascony expedition.

While he was in south Devon to inspect his fleet, it was recorded that the King visited several towns in the area, including Newton Ferrers, Ermington and Chudleigh. It was probably as a result of this royal progress that further evidence of the growing importance of Plymouth came a few years later. In 1298 the town was commanded to send two representatives to Edward I's 'Model' Parliament. It comprised Spiritual and Lay Peers, Knights of the Shire, and two burgesses from each borough, freemen whom the Sheriff of Devon considered were worthy of such an honour. The two burgesses chosen from the Borough of Sutton were William of Stoke and Nicholas Ridley. In 1304 the representatives were William Bredon and John Austin. After this, no accurate lists are known until the reign of Mary some two and a half centuries later. Plympton sent representatives to the 1295 Parliament, but Saltash remained unrepresented until the Tudor era.

Another proof of the recognition of Plymouth's importance, not least as a place of some naval significance, came a few years later. In 1302, 1308 and again in 1310 the people of the town, as well as those of Dartmouth and Teignmouth, were ordered by King Edward II to have a fleet ready to sail north to Carlisle against Robert Bruce, the King's enemy fighting for Scottish independence. As well as Plymouth, also Plympton, Modbury and Newton Ferrers were asked to prepare to join the maritime force, though in the end no fleet was ever needed.

Some municipal records survive, and Richard Tanner was Praepositus of Sutton in 1310, making him effectively the first-known holder of the office which later came to be recognised as Mayor of Plymouth. The word 'mayor' was used fairly loosely in writs and other legal documents, though strictly speaking the two offices were not exactly the same. Equivalent to a head bailiff or reeve, he was probably appointed at the annual meeting of the court leet, a manorial court which dealt with petty law and order and the administration of communal agriculture. Records exist of a Maurice Berd serving as mayor in 1370, and this is accepted as sufficient evidence that during the fourteenth century, if not earlier, the town had a governing body, including a mayor or equivalent, and representatives in Parliament.

Also throughout this time there are brief records of inquisitions concerning the rights of the King, the priors and the burgesses, and their legal relationships and prerogatives. These all indicate a desire by the people to manage their own affairs, particularly with regard to amalgamating the districts that were growing up around Sutton. One relates to the fact that the burgesses had no right to create their own market, a privilege which had been conferred on the priors by Henry III. Taking the law into their own hands, they decided to set up their own stalls in order to sell their produce. An inquisition held by the Bishop of Exeter in 1311 established that they could only legally do so as long as they erected a maximum of eighteen stalls, at a fee of a penny a year which was to be paid to the Praepositus. A further part of the agreement stipulated that they should not put up any more stalls, either there or anywhere else in the town, without a licence from the prior.

The Crown sometimes instituted enquiries into the priors' claims. In 1313, and again in 1317 and 1318, the Crown did so before the sheriff's or commissioner's sitting with juries, but with little success. The priors were confirmed in their rights as laid down in the Charter of Henry III. In 1317 the burgesses of Plymouth were at court petitioning to be granted certain waste places which belonged to the Crown in return for payment of an annual rent. This was opposed by the prior and two members of the Valletort family, who gave evidence that the town was 'not of the King's,' thus suggesting that the Crown had no jurisdiction over them. They claimed that the prior was lord of two parts of the town, and the Valletorts themselves lords of the third part. The following year, the enquiry found that it would not be to the prejudice of the King or anyone else if Sutton became a free borough.

Around the thirteenth or early fourteenth century, friars arrived in Plymouth. Friars were like monks, but instead of withdrawing from the world into their own closed society they went out to preach and help the poor. The Dominicans were called Blackfriars because of the colour of their dress, their name being perpetuated in Blackfriars Lane and Blackfriars House, Southside Street. After the dissolution of the monastery, Blackfriars House became a debtors' prison, and then a meeting house for nonconformists under Nicholas Sherwill, and in the late seventeenth century it had a congregation of Huguenot refugees. There were also Carmelites, known as Whitefriars, who lived in a building by Friary station and Franciscans, or Greyfriars, who lived in Woolster Street.

The main industry of Plympton was the export of Dartmoor tin, which was mined in the south-west valleys, mainly near the River Plym at and around Cadover Bridge. Output of Dartmoor tin was at its highest between 1160 and 1190, and the main tin port was Tavistock, though some was probably exported from Sutton and Plympton as well. Plympton remained the centre of population until around the end of the thirteenth century by which time Plymouth had overtaken it, by becoming a major exporter of fish, lead, hides, wool and cloth as well as tin, while it imported wine, iron, fruit, woad for dyeing cloth, onions, wheat and garlic, mostly from Spain and Portugal. As Plympton was anxious about losing its maritime trade to Plymouth, in 1328 it petitioned to become a stannary town (a town where tin was taken for marketing under royal supervision) as the tin could be loaded directly onto ships for export there; at Tavistock it had to be transported by road to the River Tamar before it could be shipped. Although the petition was successful, Tavistock protested angrily about the possibility of losing its stannary rights and was allowed to keep them. Plympton was therefore added as a fourth Devon stannary town, but eventually lost its trade to Sutton when the River Plym silted up with the waste from the tin-streaming.

The town increased in importance as a result of activity during the Hundred Years' War waged between 1338 and 1453, with France as the starting point for many expeditions, and played a major part in the provision of men and ships. During the siege of Calais in 1346–7, a force of about 700 ships was sent from England to France. Plymouth contributed twenty-six ships manned by over 600 men.

In 1348 Edward III's son Edward, Prince of Wales ('the Black Prince'), made Plymouth his headquarters for the campaign against France, and stayed at Plympton Priory. Seven years later he was appointed Lieutenant of Gascony, and began planning another expedition against the French. During the summer his forces were assembling at Plymouth and Southampton, and the sheriffs of Devon and Cornwall were ordered to send out hurdles and gangways to Plymouth by the middle of June, the hurdles to corral horses ashore, and gangways to get the baggage trains aboard the ships. By this time maritime trade had temporarily ceased and no ship was allowed to go to sea unless fully armed, while ships in harbour had to anchor close inshore.

In case of sudden attack, local men needed to be well armed. Fire beacons were set up to warn of the approach of invaders. Devon, Cornwall and Somerset had to provide plenty of wheat, food, wine and firewood for the forces, which numbered about 3,000, considerably more than the then total population of the town, which was only about 2,000. The ships should have been assembled by 11 June, but more were still being sought the following month, while the Prince was due to arrive in the town on 1 July, but did not do so for another three weeks. Problems connected with supplies and assembling the army, as well as strong winds at sea that summer, prevented him and the fleet from sailing until 9 September. While he was in the area he lodged again at Plympton Priory, attended by four veteran nobles who had fought at the Battle of Crecy, the Earls of Suffolk, Warwick, Oxford and Salisbury, as well as other distinguished soldiers and his chamberlain, Sir Nigel Loring. He doubtless undertook some of the planning for his campaign while at the Priory, and often rode into Plymouth in order to inspect ships, men and stores, meet local merchants, and confer with the bailiff and chief citizens.

When the English army proved victorious at the Battle of Poitiers in September 1356, Jean II, King of France, and several of his noblemen were brought in captivity to England. It is thought that conquering Prince and vanquished King sailed in separate ships from France after the signing of a truce and landed at Plymouth early in May 1357. Three weeks later they were in London, where King Jean was lodged in the Tower.

Throughout the wars Plymouth was always vulnerable to foreign invasion. The first such incident during the protracted wars was when a French fleet descended on the town, probably in 1339, and set fire to some houses. (Chroniclers vary as to the exact number of raids on Plymouth, and their dates.) A second invasion was thought to have occurred in 1350, but this time the French destroyed only a few outlying farms and possibly the hamlet of West Stonehouse, then in the parish of Maker, across the Hamoaze.

Trade was sometimes stopped by war, but throughout the rest of the time it continued to flourish. Wine from Bordeaux and La Rochelle, which were still in English hands, was trans-shipped at Plymouth for Calais and the ports of the North Sea. In 1362 the town was granted a licence to trade with Portugal, and two years later had licences to export 2,000 coloured cloths and 2,000 packs of cloth from Devon and Cornwall to Gascony and Spain. Hake, caught by trawlers around the Eddystone Rocks, was a Plymouth speciality, and in 1364 a licence was granted to export 30,000 hake from Plymouth and Mousehole to Gascony.

Though England had been victorious throughout the early years and won command of the seas through defeating the French and Castilian fleets, a reverse was suffered when the English fleet was beaten by the King of Castile in 1372. Calais and a narrow strip of coast from Bordeaux to Bayonne were all that remained of English possessions in France, and once again the English coast was open to raiders.

In 1374 Edward III sent instructions to the mayor, bailiffs and burgesses that in view of the ever-present threat of invasion and the need to protect the town, they should look carefully at their defences, survey any weaknesses the town might have, and do what they could to ensure that the people would be in a position to defend themselves against further attack. The mayor and bailiffs 'and all and singular the inhabitants of the town were to be obedient and aiding in the performance and execution of these premises', and the abbeys at Plympton, Buckfast and Tavistock had to raise men to guard their estates from the enemy. Soon after the death of Edward III in 1377 and the accession of his grandson Richard II, a boy barely ten years old, the French sent an invasion fleet to all the major ports along the southern coast of England, and Plymouth was burned and pillaged. Richard II realised that while defences could be ordered, they had to be financed. In 1378 he made a grant for its defence of six years' customs duty to the 'mayors, bailiffs, honest men and commonalty', and he granted a hundred marks a year for twenty years to be spent on constructing a wall under the direction of the prior.

In 1381 and 1385 expeditions were fitted out in Plymouth for Portugal, in order to seek new support for England against the Kings of Castile. These led to the foundation of England's oldest European alliance when Philippa of Lancaster, daughter of John of Gaunt and granddaughter of Edward III, married Joao I, King of Portugal in 1387. These expeditions to Lisbon were also to keep Castilian galleys out of the Channel.

By 1377 Plymouth had a 'taxable inhabitancy' of 4,837 persons, namely those liable for poll tax, requiring everyone above the age of fifteen to pay one shilling annually. Plymouth thus ranked as the fourth largest town in England, behind London, Bristol and York. It continued to grow steadily throughout the fifteenth century, but all new development had to be fitted within the town walls. There was expansion in the fifteenth century when the wall was extended eastwards and gates at North Street and Coxside (Sutton Road) were added. The land outside the walls was purely agricultural, with farms at such places as Pennycross, Mutley, Compton, St Budeaux and Keyham. Other farms had place names such as Tor and Venn in the Peverell area that have long since disappeared from the Plymouth map.

It is reported that the town was attacked and burnt in 1377, 1400 and 1403. No details survive of the first of these. The second was probably at the hands of James de Bourbon, Comte de la Marche, on his return from helping the Welsh in their efforts to gain independence from England. Bourbon had chased some trading vessels into the Sound and taken advantage of the opportunity to attack the town. Twelve of his ships were sunk in the harbour, and he only escaped with some difficulty.

Better documented is an attack by a considerably larger French fleet on 10 August 1403, when a force of thirty ships carrying 1,200 men, led by Sieur du Chastel of St Malo, having cast anchor in the Cattewater the previous evening, sailed into the

Plaque on the side of Mayflower House commemorating the Breton invasion of 1403.
(© Russell Parkin)

Sound up the Cattewater and landed about a mile north of the town. They marched into the town from the direction of the Whitefriars buildings, began fighting near the site of what is now Exeter Street, moved into the narrow streets and spent the night in hand-to-hand fighting, pillaging, burning and killing. Some 600 houses were said to have been plundered. The townsfolk put up a spirited fight, and the invasion lasted only one night with the French departing next day after burning much of the town, a task made easier for the enemy by the fact that most of the buildings were built of wood with thatched roofs. Afterwards part of the town was named Briton Side, later becoming Breton Side. The French also tried to penetrate the Old Town but were soon beaten off, retreated to their ships and sailed away the next morning. This invasion proved that the harbour entrance to Plymouth was well protected, but the rest of the district was not.

In the wake of this invasion, the town was soon rebuilt and began to flourish once more. After the French raids the people sent a petition to Parliament requesting permission to elect their own mayor and corporation. They wanted to build a wall around the town to protect their homes, but could do so only by buying land for the purpose, which was impossible unless they were a body corporate. As the petition was rejected, they built a wall around part of the town without official sanction.

Early in the fifteenth century a castle was built on a rocky area above the Barbican at the entrance to Sutton Harbour. A chain was stretched across the entrance to the harbour to prevent enemy ships from gaining access, and the first two towers of the castle were probably built at that time. King Henry V's Lord Chancellor, Bishop Stafford of Exeter, granted indulgences ('a remission of the temporal punishment for sin after its guilt has been forgiven') in 1416 to anybody who would offer funds to help build the walls and a further two towers. These were soon built, and the remainder was completed not long afterwards. One of the towers had Bishop Stafford's coat of arms

The Prysten (or Priest's) House, next to St Andrew's Church, built in the fifteenth century.

engraved in its stonework. When completed it had four towers, one at each corner, and thus became known as the Castle Quadrate. Since then, the towers have been shown on the city's coat of arms. The people solved the problem of maintaining the castle by apparently allocating each of the towers to one of the electoral wards of the town. Everybody had an interest in its maintenance as everyone was responsible for taking their part in the 'watch and ward' at the castle. Three aldermen and six councillors were allocated to each of the towers in time of attack, with the mayor taking position in the one overlooking the harbour entrance.

By 1610 it had become a workhouse, and was partly destroyed by fire in 1624. It was last used for defence during the siege in the Civil War, and with the planning of the Royal Citadel it became totally redundant. By 1807 the only remains were the base of one tower, measuring 30ft in diameter, and the gateway in Lambhay Street, which survived longest as it used as a dwelling. The site is today marked by Castle Street and Castle Dyke Lane, from the top of Lambhay Hill to New Street.

Plymouth's attempts at corporate independence began around 1384, partly as a result of defence measures and royal authority. King Edward's defence order had been addressed to the men of the port, and the mayor and bailiffs had to be obedient to them where such matters were concerned. In 1384 King Richard's order went to the mayor of Plymouth. Since the 1311 market agreement, the prior's steward had ridden into Plymouth on the first Monday after the feast of St Michael, 29 September, to swear in twelve of the prior's tenants, who had then elected a reeve or Prepositus. He was presented to the prior's steward, and if he proved acceptable, then took the oath. Thereafter he was head of the court which sat in Plymouth every Monday, exercising for the prior the assize of bread and ale, authority over weights and measures, millers, bakers, butchers, sellers of wine and those who brought bread in from outside the town, with jurisdiction over transgressors, collecting all debts due to the prior, market stall rents, and rendered an account of all this to the prior's agent at the end of the year. He was the town's chief magistrate, and from 1369 onwards he was known as the mayor. Though elected by his fellow townsmen, he was still acting on the prior's authority, exercising the prior's rights, and subject to the approval of the prior.

In September 1384 John Sampson was elected. He had been to Westminster in 1369 with Thomas Fishacre as one of the King's shipping advisers, and was one of the port men to whom the defence order of 1374 had been addressed. Several of the burgesses of Plymouth elected a rival, Henry Passour, who set himself up as mayor without the authority of the prior. From January 1385, he prevented John Sampson from sitting at the Monday court by force of arms. The authority he and his friends quoted was that 1374 writ which ordered the burgesses to see to the defences, and required the mayor and burgesses 'and all and singular to be obedient to them.' When the prior protested to the King, an enquiry was ordered. The jury was sworn in at a hearing at Eggbuckland in June 1385, and they found in favour of Sampson. Passour attempted to uphold his claim in the courts the following year, quoting documents from Edward III and Richard II addressed to the mayor of Sutton and Plymouth, and claiming that such forms of address were appointing the people of Plymouth to have their own mayor. However such claims had no authority against the sealed charters of the prior.

The town and its surrounding area achieved municipal independence in 1439, becoming the first town to be incorporated by Act of Parliament. As the higher parts of the Plym estuary became silted up, ships used the Cattewater moorings and the then tidal harbour at the Plym's mouth instead of Plympton. The name of the town of Sutton gradually became Plymouth instead, though the name Sutton still survives in the name of its old harbour.

In the Middle Ages wine from France and Spain was imported into Plymouth. By an Act of Richard II in 1390, Plymouth and Dover were designated the only English ports from which pilgrims could sail. Mercantile trade was established, and boosted by the Act of Incorporation which made Plymouth a free borough, with one mayor and one community, capable of owning land, the first Devon town to be thus incorporated. The first petition of Parliament was in 1411, when the people of Sutton Prior and Sutton Vautort joined forces and petitioned for the right to elect a mayor and levy taxes for defence of the area. The appeal was unsuccessful and they were advised to come to an agreement with the priory first.

In 1439 a new petition was presented to King Henry VI, setting forth the grievances of the petitioners and their request for amalgamation under one mayor of the three Suttons, namely Prior, Vautort and Raf, and freedom from the rule of Plympton Priory. The King gave his assent, and an Act of Parliament confirmed and granted the petitioners' requests.

The authorities of Plympton Priory now saw that the township which they had nurtured had come of age, and that a united borough would be better placed to withstand future attacks from outside. It was apparent that King and Parliament were in favour of incorporation. Accordingly an inquisition was held at Plympton under the Archdeacon of Totnes in January 1440. Certain details with regard to the annual rents of tenements were discussed and some rents reduced. In July 1440 the King granted Plymouth its first Charter, the main provision being that the town of Sutton Prior, the tything of Sutton Raf, and the hamlet of Sutton Vautort would become a free Borough Incorporate with one mayor. He was to be elected every year on 17 September, St Lambert's Day, or on the first Monday afterwards, and appointed on the feast of St Michael, 29 September. The priory would retain the advowson, or right of nomination or presentation to an ecclesiastical benefice of St Andrew's Church with the tithes appertaining, as well as St Nicholas Island, and three messuages or dwelling houses in Bilbury Street, Notte Street and Stillman Street respectively. It was only the second such municipal corporation in the country to be created by Act of Parliament, Hull having been the first six months earlier.

Until the time of the Reform Acts in the nineteenth century, a custom persisted that on Michaelmas Day the council would assemble at about 10 a.m. and wait for an hour before the mayor took the oath. It was a legacy from the old days, when the burgesses had to wait for the prior's officer to arrive before their choice could take office. After the oath, the mayor and corporation went in procession through the town.

The first officially-recognised holder of the position was William Ketrich. He was a Yorkshireman, and a contemporary chronicler described him as 'a little squat man, remarkable for shooting with the strong-bow, and one of the greatest satires of the time.' At his mayoral feast, he provided a pie containing several different kinds of fish, flesh and fowl, measuring 14ft by 4in. Because of its huge size, a special oven had to be built in which to bake it, and 'as big as Ketrich's pie' became a popular local phrase. His successor, Walter Clovelly, was nicknamed 'goat's face' as he had a very long beard, which he had vowed would never be cut nor shaved after his wife's death. Ketrich was not the only early mayor to achieve immortality on account of matters related with food. It was reported that James Durnford, who took office in 1455, on the first day of his mayoralty 'was taken in a fit at church.' Fortunately he made a speedy recovery, and at dinner later that day ate a fine Michaelmas goose, remarking that his illness at Mass had 'given him a passing good stomach.'

Between St Lambert's Day and Michaelmas Day the town boundaries were beaten, in order to show the new mayor and for his predecessor to remind him of the full extent of the town. It was celebrated as a holiday for the town, and in 1496 there were two gallons of wine for the mayor and his brethren. Freedom Day, as it was known, was one of the great local festivals of the year, and finished with a battle between the Old Town Boys and the Breton Boys. Old Town was by now the town within the walls, while the Breton Boys came from the suburb east of Martyn's Gate. It was a celebration of the Breton raid of 1403, and could have been a remnant of the old animosity between the town and the 'Britayns' outside their gate. At length the Freedom Day fights became too unruly, and were moved further up the hill to the area later known as Freedom Fields. When the fights descended into drunken brawls, and a particularly fierce affray occurred in 1792 when several of the participants sustained broken bones, this part of the annual celebration was discontinued.

By the mid-fourteenth century Plymouth was becoming a strong commercial centre, ruled very much by its merchants. They were given a guild in the charter of 1440, and the usual form of government of a guild (the twelve aldermen and the twenty-four councillors) was the form of the town council. In those days, everyone who ran a business or traded in the town was a member of the merchant guild. A guild meeting was a meeting of all the townsmen. The guild enforced trading regulations, saw fair business done, and ensured there was no unfair competition. Town councillors were the senior members of the guild, acting as the executive committee of the guild and of the town.

High Street, *c.* 1890, of which little now survives; what is left has been
absorbed into Buckwell Street.

Only freemen could hold office in the borough, and in 1471 the council decreed
that every freeman had to be a brother of the merchants' guild. Half-brothers paid 6*d* a
year to the guild, full brothers and aldermen 1*s*, and councillors an extra 8*d*.

By the fourteenth and fifteenth centuries the full extent of the town was still small.
There was little south of Notte Street, although the line of Southside Street ran towards
the castle, situated just above what is now the West Pier. From Notte Street another
street led up to Hoe Gate. To the west there was nothing beyond Catherine Street,
although the wall was much further out. The West Frankfort Gate was at the junction
of routes to what was then called the Sourepool and to Stonehouse. Looe Street,
Buckwell Street and the southern part of Old Town Street had recently been built.
The wall ran along the northern boundary, past Old Town Gate and then south to

Martyn's or East Gate. Breton Side, where it began on the northern shore of Sutton Pool, lay outside the wall until much later. Also outside the wall was the Carmelite Friary from which Friary station later took its name.

The manor of East Stonehouse is thought to be at least as old as Plymouth, as prehistoric and Roman remains have been found there, though not at Devonport. By the time of the Domesday Book, the manor was held by Robert the Bastard, who also held Efford. In 1368 it passed to Stephen Durnford, a merchant and landowner who owned several other estates in the area, and who gave his name to Durnford Street.

The main access to the town from the London direction was along what is now Old Laira Road, Lipson Vale, up the steep northern slope of Lipson Hill and then down the southern side to join the present Gasking Street, which much later would boast a town gate of its own. Entry into the town would have been through Martyn's Gate, by the present King's Head public house. At the time Devonport did not yet exist, and the area which it would later cover was still purely agricultural, with the manor house at Keyham Barton which overlooked Keyham Lake, which covered the area from the Hamoaze up to the base of Swilly and was crossed at the Ford, from which Ford Hill took its name. The parish church was known as Stoke Damerel, the parish itself stretching up to St Budeaux and east to the area now covered by Central Park.

As the Hundred Years' War drew towards its inglorious conclusion, the town was still required to send ships to participate in the conflict. In 1452 an order was issued for as many vessels as possible from Plymouth and other ports to rendezvous at Sandwich before the last day of February 1453. Next year the King and his councillors were intending to despatch another army to France, and he wrote to 'mayors and customers' of Plymouth, Dartmouth and Fowey:

Durnford Street, Stonehouse, *c.* 1900, named after the fourteenth-century merchant Stephen Durnford.

… preying hereby that by all the weyes and menes possible to you, ye on our behalve sture, moeve, trete and enduce with all the oweners and maisters of the shippes and vessailles that belonge unto youre porte to be ready to go.

In the end, these ships never sailed as the war ended that year. A defeated England was no longer in any financial position to pursue her claim to the throne of France.

During the Wars of the Roses, once fighting had broken out in 1455, Plymouth's sympathies lay largely with the Lancastrian cause. There were no military campaigns or pitched battles during the conflict as far south-west as Devon, but the attitudes of individual mayors, who were grateful for what Henry VI had done for the town, doubtless coloured this partisanship. Moreover the Courtenay family and Earls of Devon had always been supporters of the Lancastrian dynasty. The Bonvilles were the only local Yorkist family with any power.

Vincent Petelysden, mayor from 1456–7, attended church every Sunday morning with a red rose in his hat, to show his loyalty to the house of Lancaster, and this example was soon followed by the aldermen and burgesses. Nevertheless, the anarchy in central government engendered by the weak-minded King Henry VI and over-mighty barons around him would soon produce a strong faction in favour of the Yorkist line among the merchants and in the ports.

In 1461 the Lancastrians were defeated, Henry VI was deposed and the Earl of March took the throne, reigning as King Edward IV. According to a chronicler, this led to a quarrel between the mayor, John Paige, and Ranulph Morewill, vicar of St Andrew's:

The mayor insisted that particular prayers should be put up for the success of King Henry's arms against the rebellious Yorkists, which the vicar stubbornly refused, yet not unwisely. The mayor threatened to the King, and the vicar defied him. Yet to shew that loyalty is not confined to any party, but him that ruleth, this very mayor in the same year, feasteth the Duke of Clarence, brother to King Edward IV, right royally, here in Plymouth, and drinketh long life and a prosperous reign to King Edward IV.

Meanwhile, shortly after the decisive Yorkist victory at the Battle of Towton in Yorkshire, the King of France sent a force into Plymouth to aid the Lancastrian cause. When William Champernowne of Modbury, a Yorkist and related by marriage to the Bonvilles, sent his men towards Plymouth to repel the French, he was intercepted by Courtenay men at Yealmpton and kept out of the town. A couple of years later John Rowland, mayor between 1463 and 1466, was said to be 'a man of great interest and sway and closely attached to the House of York'; and that he was chosen as mayor 'more from fear and awe, than reverence and love.'

The Yorkists could afford to be magnanimous in victory. Plymouth and its trading position had suffered as a result of the recent upheavals during the war. When Edward IV renewed the town's charter, the annual rent to the prior of Plympton was reduced from £41 to £29 6s 8d in order to compensate for it having fallen on hard times.

William Yogge, who had been Mayor of Plymouth immediately before John Paige, took the same office again in 1470. That year the Earl of Warwick, who had been instrumental in the Yorkists' success, turned against his former friend Edward IV and took the Lancastrian side, at the same time persuading the King's brother George, Duke of Clarence, to join him. Both men landed at Plymouth with two Lancastrian nobles, the Earls of Pembroke and Oxford, and were dined in the Guildhall by Yogge.

King Henry VI was briefly restored to the throne, until Warwick was killed at the Battle of Barnet in April 1471, and a Yorkist restoration took place.

William Yogge had served as mayor four times, but after 1470 his name disappeared from the local records. In 1471 the town council passed a resolution that in future no 'foreign' man could be a freeman, followed by an entry in the town's records that John Yogge and other 'foreigns' were 'put out of their freedom.' The Yogges were a Cornish family as well as being Lancastrian supporters, and it seems that the council was now composed of Yorkists, or at least people who considered it prudent to be seen openly supporting the Yorkist cause.

Edward IV died suddenly in April 1483, and was succeeded by his twelve-year-old son as Edward V before the Lord Protector, Edward IV's brother Richard, Duke of Gloucester, declared that the kingdom would be best served by having a sovereign of mature years and took the throne as Richard III. The direct Lancastrian line had died out, but the Yorkists had a new enemy in the Tudors, represented by Henry Tudor, Earl of Richmond. From his base in Brittany, Henry was ready to organise a rising in the west, which would coincide with a series of rebellions breaking out in southern England. The plan ultimately proved to be a failure. He tried to land in Plymouth Sound, and then a few other points along the coast, but everywhere he found his way blocked by soldiers loyal to Richard. The rebels had been dispersed, and storms blew him back to Normandy. In August 1485, he landed at Milford Haven and was victorious against Richard III, who was slain at a pitched battle at Bosworth. The reign of King Henry VII, and a glorious era in the history of Plymouth, was about to begin.

three

Tudor Plymouth

By the end of the Middle Ages, Plymouth in its present-day form was starting to emerge. As the town was over 200 miles from London, and surrounded by the hardly affluent Devon rural hinterland, its economic strength depended largely on the sea. Plymouth Sound was (and still is) one of the world's largest natural harbours, and its importance lay partly in the strategic position guarding western approaches to the Channel, partly in the trading potential it offered with south-western Europe and the Atlantic. Its rise to national prominence would forever be associated with England's emergence during the next two or three centuries as a maritime power.

King Henry VII's defeat of the Yorkist dynasty and accession to the English throne brought an end to the Wars of the Roses. Sir Richard Edgcumbe, whose family were of yeoman stock from Milton Damerel, had acquired Cotehele by marriage. He was a staunch Lancastrian and supporter of the Tudors, and received several offices from the new sovereign, among them Comptroller of the Royal Household and Constable of Launceston. In 1494 he became Sheriff of Devon, and the people of Plymouth gave him presents of two sugar loaves, wine, oranges and pomegranates. In 1493 his son Piers had married Joan, heiress of the Durnford family, and she brought him the old Valletort lands at Stonehouse and Maker. They lived at the Stonehouse manor house off Durnford Street, and also probably at the old Valletort house at Church Hill, Plymouth. In the sixteenth century Piers was responsible for building Mount Edgcumbe.

Sir Richard was also given the task of being responsible for quelling any pro-Yorkist rebellion which might take place in the West Country. A few piratical followers of Lambert Simnel, first of the Yorkist pretenders to the throne, attacked the coast from Plymouth to Land's End, but their raids had little effect and they were soon driven off. A few mayors had shown loyalty to the Yorkists, but at the time of the reign of Henry VI the town remained solidly pro-Lancastrian and Tudor.

Another noted soldier who made his name in Plymouth at this time was Sir Robert Willoughby de Broke. He made himself a landed gentleman by marrying Blanche Champernowne. Originally from Dartington, the Champernownes had acquired the Valletort lands at Modbury by marriage. Sir Robert became Plymouth's first Lord High Steward and England's first Lord High Admiral.

The dawn of the Tudor era coincided with increasing prosperity in Plymouth and the surrounding area, which was reflected in a programme of church rebuilding. St Andrew's Church had initially been built around the twelfth or thirteenth century, and was partly rebuilt in 1480–1, according to an account book kept by Thomas Tregarthen, the Plymouth mayor that year, and the town's oldest surviving account book. It includes a list of sums 'assigned and granted by diverse persons to the making of the south aisle.' After 1485 the same book records money spent on the church, including stained-glass windows, stones for the north aisle and the tower, and for paving the street by the church stile. It was recorded by Leland, a sixteenth-century visitor to Plymouth, that a merchant of the town, Thomas Yogge, paid for the building of the steeple and the north aisle of the church, and that the town supplied the material. Yogge, it is assumed, was a son or some other descendant of the late Lancastrian-supporting mayor, and was so pleased to see the Yorkists finally vanquished by the Tudors that he wanted to present Plymouth with some token of his gratitude to the Almighty.

In 1497 John Cabot discovered Newfoundland with its rich stocks of fish, and soon after that Plymouth fishermen established a regular trade off the coast of Newfoundland. Fishing was now the most important industry in Plymouth. Many other goods were imported into the town including wine, fruit, sugar and paper from France and Spain. Hemp, for rope making, was imported from the Baltic, and hops from Holland. Wool and tin were exported from Plymouth. There was a coastal trade, with ships bringing in goods from other parts of England to Plymouth. Coal was brought by ship from Newcastle and grain from Eastern England.

Plymouth had a direct link with the Tudors in October 1501 when Princess Catherine of Aragon landed at the Barbican on her journey from Spain to marry

Palace Court House, where Catherine of Aragon stayed after her arrival in Plymouth in 1501. It was demolished in 1880.

Henry VII's eldest son Arthur, Prince of Wales. After her arrival she went to St Andrew's Church to give thanks for her safe arrival after a stormy voyage. She spent the next fortnight in the town, lodging in Palace Court House, the property of John Paynter, a merchant and several times Mayor of Plymouth. From the gentry and merchants she was sent gifts of oxen and sheep, and hogsheads of 'Gaston wyne' and mellow 'clarett.' Having a 'royal' in their presence was a source of much excitement in Plymouth, and the crowds were frustrated when they gathered to see their future Queen, only to find out that her duenna or chaperone, Donna Elvira Manuel, insisted that the Princess had to keep her face veiled at all times.

Plymouth still needed to maintain her defences against possible attack, particularly from the French. The Castle Quadrate covered too limited a field to be really effective. There was a period of activity around 1519 when a survey was made of the town walls, with bulwarks and gun platforms built along the edge of the Hoe cliffs to command the entrance into the Cattewater. Bishop John Voysey of Exeter offered indulgences to penitents who helped to build the walls and fortifications required, but they – or the resulting funds – were not enough to do more than create a short wall running from the west of the castle. As yet there was no financial assistance from the royal coffers.

This situation changed from around 1537 onwards when Henry VIII ordered that blockhouses, castles and platforms were to be built at various parts on the frontiers of the realm for defence purposes. Among these were what were known for some years as the Henry VIII Towers at Stonehouse and a series of works along the seafront to Lambhay Point. They also included octagonal guard towers below the level of Madeira Road and at Fisher's Nose to protect the mouth of the Plym, at the entrance to Millbay, and on Devil's Point to cover the mouth of the Tamar, both of which still survive. In earlier times such defences had been erected at the town's expense, and these were the first for which any financial assistance was provided by the Crown.

These defences were built at the right time, for in 1544 France made peace with Spain and turned against its age-old adversary, England. James Horsewell, then Mayor of Plymouth, and William Hawkins both received the King's commission to 'annoy the King's enemies.' This was another privateering venture, to inflict damage on French commerce at great profit to England. One of Hawkins's ships took a Spanish vessel, on the grounds that its cargo was French but falsely represented as Spanish. At the time a French invasion seemed imminent, and it was uncertain whether France and Spain would join forces against England. Hawkins was called before the Privy Council while the King was at Portsmouth with his fleet, and imprisoned until he had made sufficient restitution to the owner of the captured ship. However, the owner was a Spaniard who had become a naturalised Frenchman, so Hawkins could therefore justify his actions. Nevertheless a short spell in prison was not then regarded as a mark of discredit, and did his standing as a citizen no harm. He continued to land himself in minor trouble when his ship captured some Flemish goods, and again a little later when he captured a Breton ship shortly after a peace treaty had been signed. Even so, such misdemeanours – if they can be counted as such – did not prevent him from being recognised as a valued servant of the community and being regularly summoned to Parliament as Member for Plymouth.

The town was greatly affected by the Act for the Dissolution of the Monasteries in 1536 and the resulting religious changes. In 1538 the Bishop of Dover rode through the West Country closing down the friaries and smaller religious houses, dealing first with the White Friars and then the Grey Friars the next day. Their closure caused

New Street, Barbican, *c.* 1890, built in the early sixteenth century and little altered since.

little trouble, but when a further Act of 1539 closed the larger institutions, greater conflict ensued. The destruction of Plympton Priory proved particularly ruthless. Five years earlier John Howe, the last prior, had already acknowledged the King's supremacy, but this did not save the building from being confiscated and closed. It was used as a quarry, and its stone was used to build the village of Underwood. The 'lordship of the house, and all its privileges in Devon, Cornwall, Somerset and Dorset, together with the patronage of St Andrew's Church and the other religious establishments' were all transferred to the possession of Plymouth. Also included in the deed of capitulation was a Cistercian abbey near the mother church and a convent in Catherine Street.

St Andrew's Street, *c.* 1880.

The advowson of St Andrew's was also confiscated by the Crown. Accounts were written of the items of Church plate and other possessions which were disposed of at this time, such as chalices, silver crucifixes, candlesticks and precious vestments. Most, if not all of them, were sold, with the money raised going to the Treasury for the purchase of armaments.

During the rebellion which followed the establishment of the English Prayer Book, early in the reign of King Edward VI, the era known as Commocion Time, a revolt started in the West Country in April 1548 after a Commissioner was stabbed to death by a priest while trying to remove images in Helston Church. The execution of the priest, who according to different sources was either hanged or hacked to death in the streets, proved to be the catalyst for a riot. A Cornish army gathered and marched into Devon to besiege Exeter, attacking Trematon Castle on the way and some moving to Plymouth. An assault took place on the town, and guns were set up on North Hill before the Cornishmen drifted away to join the main party.

It appears that on this occasion Plymouth sided with the forces of law and order and gave short shrift to the rebels. Reports exist of a gallows being erected on Plymouth

Hoe to carry out the occasional summary execution. One Cornish traitor met such a fate there, and an audit book revealed that the executioner, John Wylstrem, was paid 6s for his work, 4d was granted to the leader of the horse dragging the hurdle bearing the doomed man along the cobbled streets to the Hoe, two poles with 'cramps of iron' were fixed to the Guildhall to bear the head and one of the quarters of the mutilated corpse, and a John Mathews received 12d for 'carrying a quarter of the traitor to Tavistock.'

In 1553, during the reign of Edward VI's successor, his eldest sister Mary, the Earl of Bedford and various other members of the nobility sailed from Plymouth to Spain to wait upon Philip, eldest son and heir of the Holy Roman Emperor, Charles V. Other historical accounts suggest that the expedition may not have taken place at all. It is more apparent, however, that in 1557 Philip, by now having married Mary although he spent little time with her, and also having become Philip II of Spain, revisited England, landing at Plymouth and dining with the mayor and Corporation in a show of hospitality costing £300. He had come primarily to seek a military alliance with England against France and the Netherlands.

In the fifteenth century Spain and Portugal had been the European powers most involved in overseas development. During the Tudor era, it became the turn of England. That Plymouth seamen had been trained in fighting the French, and that Plymouth was uniquely placed at what was in effect the gates of the English Channel and was also a suitable departure point for what was then regarded as the New World, gave the town a pre-eminence in maritime matters. It was inevitable that Plymouth should come to prominence as the home port for several successful traders or privateers, and among the first were Sir William Hawkins and his son, Sir John. Some centuries later, the concept of privateering and slave trading may seem abhorrent. By the standards of the time, however, it was not merely acceptable, but a successful enterprise to be applauded. During the sixteenth century such activities developed as a major economic activity, especially during Elizabeth I's war with Spain, and are thought to have accounted for around 10–15 per cent of England's national import values. The expeditions which departed from and returned to Plymouth made up a significant amount of this figure, and the exploits and achievements of the men responsible showed what a thin line there was between state interests and private enterprise during the Elizabethan era.

William Hawkins, master of Henry VIII's *Great Galley*, the second largest ship in the Royal Navy, in 1513 married a Trelawny family heiress and became one of the richest men in the area. He made much of his money exporting tin and wool and importing salt from France, wine from France, Portugal and Spain, and fish from Newfoundland. Plymouth had been trading with Spain and Portugal for over a century, and Hawkins had probably visited agents in Lisbon and Seville, hearing about riches being brought back to Europe from the Americas, and the Guinea coast of Africa. Sometime around 1528–30 he decided he would undertake the journey himself. He provided and commanded the *Paule of Plimouth* on a year-long voyage which included trade with Brazil and the African Guinea Coast, and in doing so he arguably became the first Englishman to trade across the Atlantic Ocean. Two more voyages to Brazil followed, and on his return in 1532 he was elected mayor, serving in the same capacity in 1538–9. In 1537 he moved to a house on the east of Kinterbury Street, facing Sutton Harbour, where his sons William and John were brought up. He sat in Parliament for Plymouth in 1547–8 and 1553–4, dying in the latter year.

William Hawkins the younger was governor of Plymouth, and served as mayor three times, in 1567–8, 1578–9 and 1587–8. In this capacity he was involved in the carrying out of orders that Plymouth should fit out seven ships, all equal to the Queen's men-o'-war, for the Spanish Armada, and he also procured a patent which gave Plymouth authority over St Nicholas Island. He died at Deptford in 1589, a year after the Armada.

His brother John, born in 1532, was to become the most famous of the Hawkins family. His early voyages were to the Canary Islands, and while undertaking these he learned that slave labour was needed in the Spanish colonies of the West Indies. In 1562, with the support of Queen Elizabeth I, he led England's first foray into the slave trade, kidnapping thousands of men and women from Sierra Leone and elsewhere in West Africa to trade in the West Indies. Although he served as Member of Parliament for the town in 1571–2, he was never mayor, and he played less part in local life than his father and brother.

Yet the achievements of the Hawkins family both at local and national level were soon to be eclipsed by those of Plymouth's most famous son of all. Francis Drake was born at Crowndale Farm, near Tavistock, around 1540. He and his family moved briefly to Kent, where he was apprenticed to the owner of a small coastal barque and traded in goods such as cloth, corn and herring along the east coast. In about 1564 he returned to Devon, where he joined the trading fleet of the Hawkins family, to whom he was related. He married Mary Newman at St Budeaux Church in 1569, though little is recorded of her except that during the next thirteen or fourteen years she saw very little of her husband, who was away from England most of the time. Legend, surely false, has it that she promised to wait seven years for him, gave up and prepared to marry another – only to find that when she and her next bridegroom were standing at the altar, a cannon ball fired by Drake promptly landed between them.

Not long after his wedding, Drake took part in one of their voyages to the West Indies. In the next few years he made several secret voyages there as preparations for a major expedition, which left Plymouth in May 1572 with the ships *Pasha* and *Swan*, his brothers John and Joseph sailing with him. They were the first Englishmen to see the Pacific Ocean across the Isthmus of Panama, and after a few skirmishes, they ambushed and captured a Spanish gold train in South America. It was to prove a costly expedition, as he lost both his brothers, one in action and the other from fever. Nevertheless he returned with a good profit, his share of the booty being an estimated £20,000, in addition to his acquisition of two small ships from the enemy. On his homecoming to Plymouth on Sunday 9 August 1573, the townsfolk were all at worship. When the word spread around that Drake was back, the mayor, Corporation and most of the other townspeople were at divine service at St Andrew's Church – but not, so the chroniclers noted, for much longer:

> At what time the news of our captain's return, brought unto his family, did so speedily passe all over the church and surpasse their minds with desire and delight to see him, that very few or none remained with the preacher, all hastening to see the evidence of God's love and blessing towards our Gracious Queen and country, by the fruite of our captain's labour and successe.

Drake probably used some of his new wealth to buy property in Notte Street, where he was listed as a merchant in 1576. Next he planned an expedition that would result in his circumnavigation of the globe, collecting ships in the Cattewater; namely *Pelican* (renamed *Golden Hind*), *Elizabeth*, *Marygold*, *Swan* and *Benedict*. They sailed in November 1577, but a storm forced them back into port for repairs and they left again

St Budeaux Church.

the following month. Their journey took them through the Magellan Strait, up the west coast of South and then North America, and decided to return via the Pacific and Indian Oceans and the Cape of Good Hope. He returned to Plymouth, well laden with treasure, in September 1580. Having put much of his booty under guard in a tower near Plymouth, he set off for London with several horses carrying generous amounts of gold, silver and pearls, much of which was deposited in the Tower of London. As a result of his newly-acquired fortune he was able to buy Buckland Abbey, a former Cistercian monastery near Plymouth that had been converted into a private estate when Henry VIII suppressed the religious houses. In April 1581 Queen Elizabeth I

Sir Francis Drake, often regarded as the greatest of the Elizabethan
seafaring heroes.

knighted him on the quarterdeck of the *Golden Hind*, moored at Deptford, and ordered
that the ship should be preserved there as a memorial of the voyage.

Several other major expeditions left Plymouth around this time, two of which were
led by Humphrey Gilbert. His first voyage in 1578, with one ship commanded by his
half-brother Walter Raleigh, was a disaster. Fierce gales in September forced the ships
back to Plymouth and they started out again two months later. This time a Spanish
fleet caught them and dispersed them off Cape Verde. On a second attempt in 1583
Gilbert reached Newfoundland, but on his way home the ships were overwhelmed by
a storm near the Azores. Other expeditions followed, by William Hawkins, Sir Richard
Grenville and more by Drake, all provisioned and fitted out in Plymouth, which grew
in prosperity and prestige as a result.

Drake's involvement in local life was infrequent. It was thought that the aldermen
and burgesses of Plymouth might find themselves abandoned by their most prominent
citizen, and they therefore named him mayor for a term beginning in September 1581,
in order to try and persuade him to stay in the town more. However he did little if

anything for Plymouth during that time, and his only achievement appears to have been creating a 'newe compasse made upon the Hawe,' perhaps a reference to a new wall built adjoining the castle on Plymouth Hoe.

In 1586, around £280 was spent on fortifying St Nicholas Island, which was the site of the headquarters of Sir Arthur Champernowne, a former Vice-Admiral of Devon. It was seen as the key to the whole harbour of Plymouth, and armour for 350 men was stored there. Drake gave orders that a watch on the harbour should be kept nightly on the Hoe, treating Plymouth as if it was a garrison town and ever vulnerable to invasion. It is said that he also mounted a guard on the island, which thus became known as Drake's Island. He helped the mayor in an appeal to the Queen for aid in building a fort on the Hoe, where the Citadel now stands. The town walls were also repaired at around this time, and extended at the eastern end to enclose Breton Side, from Martyn's Gate to Coxside. In 1586 an order was issued that townsmen who did not do their duty or provide efficient substitutes for day or night watch were liable to be fined. A year later the Corporation ordered that all who, on any attack being offered by the enemy, 'should absent themselves or any way withdraw themselves out of the town, against their duty and allegiance, should forfeit all their goods and chattels within the liberty, be utterly disfranchised, never restored, and never allowed again to dwell therein.'

When Elizabeth I called a parliament in November 1584, the Water Bill for Plymouth was already prepared for presentation, aiming to provide a supply of water for naval and merchant shipping, and for fire fighting in Plymouth, to scour Sutton Harbour of silt, and to improve the poor quality of land on Dartmoor adjacent to the proposed leat. Large fleets tended to exhaust the local supplies and parties of seamen had to be sent to the brooks flowing down to Pennycomequick and Lipson. The Bill was passed to a select committee chaired by Drake for consideration, and he proposed an additional clause stating that mills could be erected and operated on the banks of the leat. It gained royal assent and was passed as an Act in 1585, 'for the Preservation of the Haven of Plymouth.' The town now had authority to tap the waters of the River Meavy near Tavistock and bring the water to the port by a leat or open waterway.

St Nicholas Island, later Drake's Island, from Plymouth Sound.

An entrance to the Drake's Island garrison.

However, the project was delayed by Drake's other activities, not least his next expedition to the Indies, and his action against Spain which resulted in his finest hour. A conspiracy to assassinate Queen Elizabeth and place her cousin Mary Queen of Scots on the throne in her place, known as the 'Babington plot', had been discovered and resulted in the execution of fourteen of those responsible. The shaken Queen was convinced that King Philip of Spain intended to invade the country, and she gave Drake permission to raise a fleet and take the King of Spain on in his own harbours. He sailed in April 1587, just too late to receive the messenger from Plymouth whom she had sent with a cancellation of her order. About ten weeks later he returned, having captured and pillaged several Spanish ships at sea, raided Cadiz harbour, and brought back a casket of magnificent jewels for Her Majesty. While on his mission he had gathered sufficient information to show conclusively that the Spanish government was seriously preparing to invade England. He asked for permission to repeat his raids, something she expressly forbade him to do; had she allowed him his own way, the Spanish Armada would probably never have sailed.

Thanks to Drake, England was well aware of the dangers of Spanish invasion. In the early months of 1588 Plymouth Sound and the Cattewater were full of ships, and the fleet put to sea several times to try and destroy the Spanish fleet in their own waters, but were constantly frustrated by bad weather. In May 1588 Drake was summoned to London, where he was told that Lord Howard of Effingham was to be commander of the English fleet, while Drake himself could have the post of second in command. Howard joined Drake at Plymouth later that month, where the latter explained his plan to attack the Spanish fleet in Spanish waters. In full agreement with this scheme, twice Howard tried to take his fleet towards the Spanish coast, but storms forced him back to port each time. On 19 July word arrived that the Armada had been sighted off the Lizard heading towards Plymouth. Legend has it that Drake was on Plymouth Hoe, completing his game of bowls while waiting for the tide and winds to change before sailing to attack the enemy. Rather than going to his ship immediately, he is supposed to have remarked that there was plenty of time to finish the game and then to finish the Spaniards. Whether the story has any factual basis is unknown, but from what is known of his impatience and a passionate desire to send the enemy packing, it is unlikely.

The successful manoeuvre which made victory most probable involved sailing as far west and windward of the Spanish fleet as they could, with Drake and his smaller ships then harrying the Spanish line, giving it little chance to retaliate. There was a striking difference between both naval forces, with the Spaniards boasting a number of large ships in contrast to the smaller English vessels which sailed faster, were easier to manoeuvre, and were better equipped with cannon capable of greater range. During a skilled campaign at sea lasting several days Drake, Hawkins and Howard attacked the Armada, stormy seas drove it northwards round the coast of Scotland, at which stage the British fleet broke off its pursuit. It could not have continued any further, for the fleet was in a bad state, with the men exhausted and ill. They were also starving, as the provisions they had received at Plymouth on 23 June had only been intended to last a month but in fact were all they had for seven weeks. Moved by the misfortunes of their men, Hawkins and Drake paid for extra food supplies themselves as no further funds were forthcoming from the Treasury, and they also founded what became known as the Greenwich Hospital Fund, to provide a hospital for men wounded or incapacitated in the Armada campaign, and then for all other seamen wounded in the course of their duty.

Nevertheless Plymouth would never forget this victory over the Spanish Armada. For many years the bells of St Andrew's were rung each year on the Saturday night before the anniversary, and on the Sunday, the mayor and Corporation marched to church on Sunday to take part in a special thanksgiving service.

In 1589 Drake was ordered on a punitive expedition to Portugal, to destroy any remaining ships which had taken part in the Armada, as well as give support to rebels in Lisbon against King Philip II of Spain. The venture was a failure, resulting in the loss of over 12,000 lives and twenty ships.

It may or may not have been coincidence that soon after this some more attention was paid to domestic matters, namely the water supply. During Drake's mayoralty, an idea for a water leat was considered by the Corporation of Plymouth. Work began in December 1590 and the water began to flow on 24 April 1591. The leat was seventeen miles long, a simple ditch about 6ft wide and 2ft deep. It had to wait a century before

The Armada Memorial, Plymouth Hoe, unveiled in 1890.

getting a hard floor and cut granite sides. The head weir is now covered by Burrator reservoir. Plymouth gave him £200 to pay for the construction of the leat, and £100 with which to compensate the owners of land through which the leat passed.

Plymouth marked the first flowing of water to the town with celebrations. Messengers took an invitation to Drake at Buckland Abbey and to Mr Harris, another Member of Parliament for Plymouth. Wine and other provisions were assembled, and four trumpeters rode out on hired horses. The present and former mayors, Walter Pepperell and John Blythman, rode with the aldermen and councillors and their wives to the head weir, to meet Harris and Drake. Presents were given to James and Robert Lampen, who had planned the course of the leat and built it; to the foremen, and to the rector of Meavy. He blessed the enterprise, the trumpets were sounded, the sluice was opened and water began to flow to Plymouth, where it was greeted with a burst of gunfire and a celebratory dinner. Drake and all the dignitaries who had been at Head Weir for the opening rode back to the dinner, and it was assumed that they took the route over Yennadon and Roborough Down to Plymouth, keeping pace with the water. A legend, which may contain a germ of truth, tells of Drake riding proudly into the town on a white horse, with water flowing at the horse's tail.

Once the water was in Plymouth, it was piped, and in 1602 the Corporation ordered that nobody should pipe water into his house without permission. Although a severe frost in the winter of 1607/8 burst many of the pipes, by 1608 thirty-eight houses were connected.

Although the Armada had been decisively defeated and Spain was now no longer a threat, the town was always acutely conscious of its vulnerability to the activities of spies. In July 1591 it was rumoured that ten seminary priests and Jesuits had been landed in a creek near Plymouth by a London merchant who had received £60 for his trouble. In February 1593 John Sparke wrote to the Privy Council that many of the people were leaving, as they had heard that the Spaniards were intending to burn the town during the summer.

Nevertheless, when Drake was Member of Parliament for Plymouth in 1593, he decided that the town's defences should be further strengthened. It was vulnerable to further Spanish attacks and reprisals from the King of Spain, and as Drake informed Queen Elizabeth, it was 'not defended by any fort or rampier.' When its captains were away from the town, there was 'a chronic state of alarm.' In December 1591 a local commission, which included Drake, was asked to recommend whether it would be best to build a fort in or near the town, or to build a wall around it. Within a few months the commission had produced a plan showing Plymouth entirely surrounded by a wall and ditch with three gates and nine bulwarks, as well as an elaborate Citadel on the Hoe. This latter edifice was designed to overlook the Sound and command the entrance to the Cattewater and so to Sutton Pool.

At this time the Hoe was still just a barren limestone ridge, covered with gorse, scrub and rough pasture, about 1,200 yards long and rising to a height of 100ft above sea level. It formed a natural lookout place from which could be seen to the south the Sound and its approaches. To the north was a view of scattered farms and the landward approaches to Plymouth, ending in the panorama of Dartmoor Forest about fifteen miles away. The only building of importance there was St Catherine's Chapel at the eastern end, built towards the end of the Hundred Years' War by the Black Prince or his followers, and demolished after the Citadel was built. Its tower was important as a landmark, as a lighthouse for shipping, and as a station for a lookout.

Elizabethan House, on the right-hand side, New Street, built about 1600.

Looe Street, shortly before the houses on the left were demolished, *c.* 1890.

The Privy Council then sent to Plymouth an experienced military engineer, Robert Adams, who stayed in the area for about eighteen months. He was instructed to study the commission's plans and to confer particularly with Arthur Champernowne. With the help of local contractors and workmen they were to estimate the cost of the work. In April 1592 Adams wrote to the Privy Council that he had discussed the work with Champernowne and that 'some difference, howbeit not great, fell out betweene us.' Champernowne wanted to defend the town with a wall, whereas Adams recommended building a fort, seventy-five perches (about 450 yards) in circuit, on the high ground of the Hoe. In his opinion, to wall the town would be too expensive. Alternatively, Adams was prepared to consider a low wall 10ft high on the more vulnerable west and north sides of the town. In the event of a siege, it was assumed that the people would withdraw to the security of the fort. Nevertheless in 1599 and 1601, during the threat of Spanish invasion, they refused to do so, preferring instead to stay in their homes. Adams decided that the defence of the anchorage and the harbour was the first priority rather than that of the town.

The Privy Council accepted Adams's plan, and to finance it, in May 1592 they imposed a duty on the export of pilchards from Plymouth, the principal source of wealth at the time. This duty was to continue yearly until the town was fully fortified, by enclosing it with a ditch, wall, bulwarks and other defences towards the sea. £100 per annum was allocated from the customs revenue of Devon and Cornwall towards the building, and voluntary contributions were invited from local merchants and others who would benefit from the protection of the fort.

Royal Citadel Gate, built in 1670, photographed in 1924.

In 1596, a few months after Adams' death, a garrison was recruited. Sir Ferdinando Gorges was appointed its first captain, and he organised the garrison of the fort and the local militia to face threats of invasion. This brought protests from those in the town whose people regarded the militia as a protection for their families and property rather than a force for the defence of the fort and the Sound, and his problems were compounded by the government's failure to pay for his men and for the maintenance of defences. His share in privateering ventures relieved his financial problems, and the fort was completed by 1598. It was shown that the Privy Council was unwilling to provide money for regular maintenance and repair of the fort, although when invasion threatened the Crown was prepared to contribute to defences designed to protect the anchorage in the Cattewater and the shipping in Sutton Pool. It was reluctant to make a similar contribution to the defences of the town, where the people would have to provide adequately for such fortifications as they believed to be necessary.

In 1601 Gorges was implicated in the rebellion of the Earl of Essex against Queen Elizabeth I. He was imprisoned as a result and lost his command, but he was later pardoned by the Queen and restored to his position at Plymouth by James I. (In 1629 he handed over the captaincy of Plymouth Fort to Sir James Bagge.)

There were more expeditions against Spain, not all of them successful. It was inevitable that Drake should still want to take part. His seafaring days were not yet over, though his last venture was destined to be the least successful of all. In August 1595 he and Sir John Hawkins left Plymouth in joint command of an expedition to Panama, but both men were ageing and in poor health. There were arguments between the cautious Hawkins and the reckless Drake. Many of the men were unwell; soon after they anchored at Puerto Rico Hawkins died of fever in November, and Drake followed him in January 1596. Both men were buried at sea.

It was almost the end of the Elizabethan age of expeditions, and just one remained. In the spring of 1596 one more was put together by Sir Walter Raleigh, a nephew of Drake, in concert with the Earl of Essex, Lord High Admiral Howard and Sir Thomas Howard. Between them they gathered four squadrons, twenty-four Dutch ships, and nearly 150 English ships. To muster a sufficient force of men the press gangs went round the town, and Essex executed several conscripted landlubbers on the Hoe who tried to escape, as an example to the others. They sailed from Plymouth on 3 June. On the journey there were numerous petty jealousies, hatreds and bitter arguments between the leaders, especially between Raleigh and Essex. Despite this, the expedition met with some success. At Cadiz, Raleigh threatened the Spanish ship *St Philip*, whereupon the crew set fire to their ships and jumped overboard rather than fall into the hands of the English. It was a heavy blow to Spanish prestige, but an undaunted King Philip set about trying to assemble another fleet in order to try and attack the English. Within two years he was dead, and his Protestant Tudor contemporary Queen Elizabeth outlived him by only five years. The golden age of Anglo-Spanish rivalry in which Plymouth had played such a significant role was over.

Throughout the sixteenth century Plymouth had expanded fast. Between 1532 and 1600 the town nearly doubled in size, and its status as the south-west's main port became unassailable. Its main streets, in the process of being built, were clustered around Sutton Pool, but spread gradually towards Old Town. The overhanging upper storeys of houses, with diamond latticed windows supported by carved corbels, made the streets dark but offered protection against the weather. The larger, grander houses had broad staircases, the smaller ones pole staircases made from old ships' masts, the steps woven in a spiral around it, and these were the houses in which merchants and sea captains lived. Apprentices lived in tenements at the back of merchants' houses while fishermen and poorer people lived in smaller houses, generally nearer the quay.

Stonehouse was expanding, due partly to the Durnford family who built a manor house, Stone Hall, thus leading the way for others to build houses in the area, and partly because the monks were building there and regarded Stonehouse as a port from which they could ship their products when they had lost their rights to do so from Plymouth on its incorporation.

As for principal roads in Plymouth, there were two routes to Stonehouse, one via the present Citadel Road route, the other from Frankfort Gate along Stonehouse Lane, avoiding marshes to the south. Most occupations were concerned with the sea and shipping. Since the establishment of the Navy Board in the later years of Henry VIII's reign, shipbuilding had started to become a major industry. Although it was mainly other naval centres in the south and south-east which benefited at first, Plymouth soon began to play a role, and ships were first built along the shores of the Cattewater. During the next century, this would account for a major part of the town's industry. As for other commerce, the main imports at this time included wine, linen, cloth and iron ore.

In 1600 Plymouth was granted a new charter by the Queen which clarified the town's legal rights. It made the ex-mayor a Justice of the Peace in addition to the mayor and recorder, gave the town the right to have its own prison, and excluded the town from authority of the Justices of Devon. By making the mayor Clerk of the Market, it gave him control of all trading in the town.

During the Tudor era, Plymouth had regarded itself as very much at one with the English ruling dynasty. In the Stuart age, as events would prove, its loyalty would be less easily taken for granted.

four

Stuart Plymouth

By the beginning of the Stuart era, Plymouth had become a very successful trading port, though its status was soon to be sorely tested and prosperity threatened by the upheavals of the Civil War. Both Plymouth and Dartmouth relied to some extent on a profitable fishing trade with Newfoundland. Plymouth had had fifty ships in the business in 1594, and sixty in 1631, averaging about 100 tons each, with a crew of about forty men, therefore employing about 2,400 altogether. These vessels sailed to Newfoundland every spring, erected wooden platforms on the shore where the fish were treated, and returned with their catches in August. Some of these ships did not return directly to Plymouth, but instead went first to Spanish and Mediterranean ports, selling the fish and buying local goods before they returned home. Plymouth's other imports included wine, salt, fruit, sugar, iron ore, linen and paper, mostly from France, Spain and the Baltic countries, while exports included woollen goods and metals. Much of the tin mined on Dartmoor and some West Country lead passed through Plymouth, although by the early seventeenth century tin production was falling.

As a major rural industry since the Middle Ages, wool was produced throughout most of the South West. Like east Devon and Somerset, which tended to use Exeter and Dartmouth for exporting, Dartmoor had large flocks of sheep, and weaving was another cottage industry along the southern edges of the moor, while Tavistock, Buckfastleigh and Ashburton were also woollen towns, and east Cornwall was a major spinning area. Plymouth was strategically placed to export a reasonable share from all of these, and the volume of trade increased over the years, with markets including the Atlantic islands, Spain, France and the Low Countries.

Plymouth still imported many goods, the major commodities early in the seventeenth century being wine, salt, paper, pitch, canvas and linen from France; iron ore, fruit and sugar from Spain and the Canaries; rye from Germany; and hops from Holland. Much of this was for local use, though some was shipped into coasting vessels for other English ports. Coal from Newcastle and South Wales, grain from the east coast and all the town's needs came in by sea from the ports where they were available.

The age of the great explorers and privateers had largely come to an end with the passing of Elizabethan England, but there was one ignominious last chapter to be written. Shortly after his accession to the throne in 1603, King James had Sir Walter Raleigh, a cousin of Sir Francis Drake, charged with treason on spurious grounds. Raleigh was sentenced to death but then reprieved and held in the Tower of London for thirteen years, then released in 1616 on condition that he undertook another voyage to Guiana and returned with gold. Once he was given his liberty, Raleigh put together an ill-prepared expedition consisting of seven ships, which sailed from Plymouth in June 1617. The voyage was a dismal failure; he lost most of his men (including his son) and ships, and returned to Plymouth twelve months later, ill and bitterly discouraged. He was met by his cousin Sir Lewis Stukeley, Vice-Admiral of Devon, who had been given orders to arrest him. While staying in Plymouth, in effect under open arrest, Raleigh briefly considered escaping to France but decided that to do so would compromise his integrity. His end turned out to be all too inevitable. He was taken to London, given a show trial, found guilty of planning to foment war between England and Spain, abandoning his men and betraying his King, and was sent to the scaffold in October 1618.

King James had none of his predecessor's appetite for facing naval enemies head on. During his reign Algerine pirates sailed the Channel, coming to the south coast and at Plymouth raiding ships, fishing boats, and carrying people into captivity, holding them to ransom until the money was paid or they died. The King turned a blind eye until 1619 when Sir Ferdinando Gorges, governor of the fortress of Plymouth, declared war on the Turks. He planned to raise a fleet by placing levies on ports, the largest being on Bristol and Plymouth. In the autumn of 1620 an expedition under Admiral Sir Robert Mansell, with Sir Richard Hawkins as his Vice-Admiral, assembled in Plymouth harbour before attempting, but ultimately failing, to take action against the pirates.

A number of Calvinists had moved to Holland in 1607 to practise their religion in freedom and became non-conformists, but later decided to move to the New World where they could follow their own religion without interference. With a licence from the London Co. of Virginia they chartered two ships, *Mayflower* and *Speedwell*, in which they could cross the Atlantic. The emigrants had settled in Southampton where a party of English sympathisers joined them, put into Dartmouth for repairs, and again into Plymouth as *Speedwell* was leaking badly. It was apparent that she would not be ready for the voyage unless they were prepared to accept a long delay. Making a decision that *Mayflower* would sail alone, on 6 September 1620 the 102 passengers left Plymouth (from the place on the Barbican known to posterity as the Mayflower Pier) for America. They reached Cape Cod on 9 November and after the first winter, during which about half of them died of disease or starvation, established a permanent settlement.

In 1612 William Lawrence, a merchant in Vauxhall Street, died and left £100 in his will for the building of an orphanage, and three years later the Orphan's Aid was built in Catherine Street. Almshouses were built in Basket Street in 1628, and in 1630 more money was raised to build the Hospital of Poor's Portion nearby. It was probably the first proper workhouse built in England, and the need for its existence may be regarded as a comment on the distress left by Charles's wars with France and Spain.

To a certain extent the Pilgrim Fathers' voyage from Plymouth was a reflection of the town's support for nonconformists and all those unwilling to blindly accept the old established order. Soon after his accession to the throne, King Charles urgently needed additional funds, as he was planning an expedition against Cadiz. Ninety ships were assembled in Plymouth Sound and 10,000 soldiers on the Hoe. King Charles, Queen Henrietta Maria and the Court came to the town and reviewed the army on Roborough Down. The King knighted James Bagge, a former mayor and Member of Parliament for Plymouth, and charged him with fitting out the fleet. However, it was poorly equipped, the men were badly fed and the expedition was a failure. Two days after it sailed from Plymouth it returned in complete disorder. A week later it sailed a second time, but failed to take Cadiz or the Spanish treasure fleet, and within a few weeks ships were returning ignominiously to Plymouth.

The Mayflower Steps, Barbican, from which the ship of the same name sailed in 1620. (© Kim Van der Kiste)

The Barbican, with the Mayflower memorial in the background. (Courtesy of M. Richards)

Island House, *c.* 1900.

Island House, showing a plaque recording the names of all the pilgrims who sailed aboard the *Mayflower* in 1620. (© Kim Van der Kiste)

Basket Street, *c.* 1870.

The army was ordered into billets in the town, the soldiers half-naked, plague-ridden and starving. An outbreak of plague was rife, with people fleeing the town and therefore inadvertently spreading the epidemic around neighbouring communities. By June 1632 it was reported that the disease had spread so far around the area that all commerce in Plymouth had ceased, and local government was close to collapse. By July there were only two surviving aldermen left in the town, and not one single constable. The fleet began to leave around this time but the soldiers stayed until September, many of them too weak to carry their muskets by the time they left. An estimated 2,000 people died during the period, about a quarter of Plymouth's total population.

The failure of the naval expedition was ascribed partly to poor command, and also to a suspicion that Bagge had diverted much of the funds intended for the fleet into his own pocket; similar expeditions to, and raids on, France on Rochelle and Ile de Rhé, ended in similar ignominy. Plymouth was never thereafter well-disposed towards the hapless King Charles, who would soon find few allies in the West Country at a time when he needed them the most.

As if this was not enough, Plymothians quarrelled with the Crown over the appointment of the vicars of St Andrew's Church. Queen Elizabeth I had given authority to appoint the St Andrew's vicar to the mayor and Corporation, on condition that they found fit persons to serve the Church and maintained a free grammar school. In 1631 a new vicar was required to succeed the elderly, and evidently dying, Revd Henry Wallis, and the Corporation chose Thomas Ford, vicar of Brixton, but as he was a staunch Puritan, the King ordered that he should not be admitted. After Wallis died in 1632 another Puritan, Alexander Grosse, was chosen. The Bishop of Exeter refused to institute him, so Plymouth nominated Ford a second time. The King again vetoed the choice and in his place appointed the fervent Royalist Dr Aaron Wilson. He held the living for ten years, during which time he had frequent differences with the people of the town.

This led to demands that Plymouth should be divided into two parishes, and permission was sought to build a second church in the town, on the grounds that a steadily increasing population made it necessary. This was granted in 1640, on condition that the new church was named Charles Church, and next year it received royal assent by Act of Parliament. For years there was debate as to whether the church was dedicated to 'Charles, Saint Charles, or Charles the Martyr', but the wording of the Act explicitly said that the new church to be built 'shall be called Charles Church.' 'Charles the Martyr' was King Charles, but only after his execution, eight years later. It is thought that the 'Martyr' prefix originated with a zealous parish clerk, and that this designation was officially expunged from church records in 1868. Building started immediately, at the town's expense, on a site on the north-east of the built-up area. It had reached roof level in 1643 when the siege of Plymouth during the Civil War took place and further work was suspended. A canvas roof was hastily erected and the first service was held towards the end of the year by the Presbyterian chaplain to the garrison. Meanwhile, soon after the outbreak of war, Dr Wilson was seized, imprisoned and sent away to Portsmouth.

Plymouth supported Parliament in the Civil War but most of the rest of south-west of England was fervently Royalist. The Royalist leader in the west, Sir Ralph Hopton, attacked the town at the end of 1642, and cut off the water supply, but he was eventually repelled. Early the next year, an order was made for the extension of the town defences. Efforts were concentrated on building a line of stockaded earthworks with a ditch across the high ground between the indented creeks of Laira and Pennycomequick, with forts at points including New-work (now Eldad), Lipson, Cattedown and Prince Rock.

In August 1643 Colonel John Digby succeeded Hopton as Royalist commander. Sir Alexander Carew, then in command of Drake's Island, was suspected of communicating with the Royalists at Mount Edgcumbe. A party was sent to arrest him but the garrison was already holding him prisoner; he was sent to London and executed for high treason. Colonel James Wardlaw was then appointed Commander-in-Chief, assisted by Colonel William Gould. In September the King's nephew, Prince Maurice, marched on Plymouth with five regiments of horse and nine of foot. He stationed these at Plymstock, Tamerton, Mount Edgcumbe and Cawsand, making his headquarters at Widey Court. Fort Stamford, on the east side of the Cattewater, was attacked by the Royalists for over a fortnight, during which it changed hands several times before finally falling. Colonel Gould was injured in a skirmish, and the Royalist cannon at Stamford could now bombard the Hoe, but failed to cause any damage. Royalist cannon at Oreston already controlled the entrance to Sutton Harbour and guns on Mount Edgcumbe dominated Stonehouse Creek. Millbay was then the only free harbour and the defences on Drake's Island were vital to the town's survival.

The loss of Fort Stamford strengthened the town's resolve, and its inhabitants were united in one cause – the defence of Plymouth. When asked by Prince Maurice to surrender they refused, and drew up a solemn vow and covenant for the defence of the town. Probably the town's greatest day of the war was on 3 December 1643, when

A map of Plymouth defences during the Civil War, 1643.

Widey Court, headquarters of King Charles I while in Plymouth during the Civil War. It was demolished in 1954.

The Sabbath Day Fight Memorial, Freedom Fields Park, commemorating the battle of 3 December 1643. (© M. Richards)

the people successfully fought off an attack by Prince Maurice's army. The Prince and his party had advanced around Lipson Creek from Compton Village and then down the narrow valley from Eggbuckland. Those who were defending Lipson Fort were outnumbered and drew back to Freedom Fields, but the town rallied and with Colonel Gould leading the attack, the Royalists had to withdraw. Their retreat soon became a panic, especially as the tide had now filled Lipson Creek and several horsemen were drowned while attempting to cross. The Sabbath Day Fight is commemorated by a memorial in Freedom Fields Park.

A further attack at Maudlyn Fort on 20 December, which cost the Royalists dearly, persuaded Prince Maurice to raise the siege, but the town only had temporary relief from attack as the blockade was still in force. The Prince gave an order to the constables of Eggbuckland and St Budeaux to guard against the relief of Plymouth. Early in 1644

Gould replaced Wardlaw as governor, and Digby was succeeded as Royalist commander by Sir Richard Grenville. Irritated by the town's refusal to surrender, Grenville attacked the country houses of Parliamentarians, hanged villagers, and treated prisoners badly. Gould died in spring 1644 and was replaced by Colonel Martin, who kept up a strong offensive against the Royalists.

In September 1644 the King marched on Plymouth in person, camped at Roborough and demanded surrender by a summons from his court at Widey. After he had made a few daily sorties around Hartley Hill, which gave an impression of dithering, he and his army attacked in a pincer movement at Pennycomequick and Millbridge, but was driven back with large casualties. The following day he and Prince Maurice rode away, leaving Grenville in sole charge. A final major attack was launched on the town in January 1645 when Grenville led a force of 6,000 against the entire defensive line and took Maudlyn Fort, but soon afterwards the Royalists were being pursued down the hill at Mutley Plain. The King's cause was collapsing, and in January 1646 Grenville withdrew. In March Oliver Cromwell and General Sir Thomas Fairfax were welcomed into the town as the Civil War ended. Both men were received with a 300-gun salute as they visited the fort and other defences on the Hoe.

Plymouth had suffered as a result of the siege, with parish registers of St Andrew's showing over 3,000 deaths registered during the first few months alone. Some years later it was estimated that perhaps as many as 8,000 deaths could be attributed to the onslaught, 'that in three years or so a number greater than the population of the town was swept away.' The town was impoverished with food having run short, and soldiers' wages unpaid. A large amount of money had been borrowed by the committee of defence from merchants, civic leaders and many others. Many major houses had been damaged, with gardens, orchards and cultivated land ravaged. The Royalist gentry were still restless, and made plans to capture Plymouth in the event of any rebellion, but these plans leaked out and Sir John Grenville, leader of the local Royalist group, was gaoled. After an abortive uprising in March 1655 the town responded by constructing defences at North Hill.

Domestic industry had briefly been brought almost to a standstill, while foreign trade had virtually ceased, and the American colonists, suddenly deprived of support and trade, had built up their own fishing fleets, and were now trading among themselves and with the British colonies. A new Navigation Act of 1651, reinforcing a longstanding principle of government policy that English trade should be carried in English vessels, banned third party countries' ships from transporting goods from a country elsewhere in Europe to England. This legislation was aimed particularly at the Dutch, who then controlled a large section of Europe's international trade and even much of England's coastal shipping. Since the Netherlands produced very few goods itself, it excluded the Dutch from essentially all trade with England.

It was a contributory cause of the first Dutch war, a conflict which lasted from 1652 to 1654 and resulted in British victory, destroying attempts by the Netherlands to dominate world trade. Plymouth played only a minor part in the fighting, which was concentrated at the eastern end of the Channel, but this war, and a succeeding one with Spain, brought the town additional employment with fitting and provisioning ships. As the navy was seen to increase in prestige through victory over foreign powers, so did Plymouth's importance as one of the major naval centres outside the south-east develop accordingly, as a base not only for the fleet but also for convoys to the New World, the Mediterranean and the East.

The still incomplete Charles Church had been first used in 1643, with a service held by the garrison's Presbyterian chaplain, probably Francis Porter, who served as vicar from 1643 to 1665. Building work continued after the Civil War, and it was completed in 1657 or 1658. The tower was dated 1657, consecrated by the Bishop of Exeter, Seth Ward, on 2 September 1665 and the parish of Charles was created. The first spire, a wooden one, covered with lead, was built around 1707. For some years St Andrew's was known in Plymouth as the old church, and Charles Church as the new church.

After the death of Cromwell in September 1658, there was widespread fear that the government of the country might fall into the hands of a motley coalition of Quakers, Anabaptists and group of unsavoury revolutionaries. Even most of the Parliamentarians believed that it would be in the national interest to restore the monarchy. In 1660 William Morice, who had just become governor of Plymouth, was one of several prominent men who helped to restore King Charles I's son and heir to the throne as Charles II. Morice helped to arrange a vital meeting between Monck and Sir John Grenville, an emissary of the King in exile, and for his services he was later appointed Secretary of State and awarded a knighthood by the King. John Maynard, the King's Sergeant-in-Law, was also knighted and sat as Member of Parliament for Plymouth for the next thirty years. Morice briefly served in a similar capacity, but retired into private life in 1668, saying angrily that the King was 'debauching the nation.' Sir John Grenville was created Earl of Bath in 1661 and appointed Governor of Plymouth.

During the months following Cromwell's death an acute shortage of money had turned many seamen strongly against the Commonwealth. Some ships' crews had been unpaid for four years by 1660, and in Plymouth the agent victualler reported that there were six ships in the Sound with starving crews, six more were expected and that his credit was exhausted. Plymouth might have been Puritan in sentiment, and had little love for King Charles I, nevertheless, the restoration of the monarchy was seen as offering a hope for better times in return for a compromise on religious questions. It was not forgotten that the Puritan Corporation had usurped from the freemen and freeholders of Plymouth the right to elect Members of Parliament to represent the borough, the privilege of electing the mayor and other officers, and the power of admission to the freedom of the town.

Although Plymouth welcomed the restoration of the monarchy, it was apprehensive about its future, and well aware that it might pay a price for its pro-parliamentary stance during the war. Captain Westall, a Royalist spy, reported that in Plymouth some Fifth Monarchy men were encouraging the Presbyterians in resisting Prayer Book rule, and that 'several old sea captains were determined that the Common Prayer should not come into St Andrew's Church.' When the Royalist Parliament passed the Corporation Act of 1661, designed for the express purpose of restricting public offices in England to members of the Church of England, commissioners were sent to evict the mayor, William Allen, his aldermen and councillors, and put in his place their own man, William Jennens. The 1662 Act of Uniformity, which required the use of all the rites and ceremonies in the Book of Common Prayer in Church of England services, was vigorously enacted. George Hughes, vicar of St Andrew's, and his lecturer, Thomas Martyn, were seized a week before St Bartholomew's Day, 24 August, and taken to Drake's Island as state prisoners. They were replaced by King's men, though Francis Porter of Charles Church kept his position. Sent to the same prison were General Lambert and James Harrington, against whom a false charge of conspiracy was brought. Abraham Cheare, a respected Baptist minister, was arrested for 'encouraging religious assemblies' and sent to Exeter gaol. He was released after three months but re-arrested, held again at Exeter for three years, released and allowed to return to his home at Plymouth, but arrested and imprisoned again, first in a cell under the Guildhall and then on Drake's Island, where he became ill and died in 1668.

King Charles's extravagance and a need for extra funds placed him on a collision course with Holland. The capture of Dutch colonial settlements in the long run was tempting, despite the fear that the French might be dragged into war against England. In April 1664 Parliament formally denounced the Dutch as the major impediment to commercial expansion, and following several raids by Dutch and English seaman in the West Indies, East Indies, the Mediterranean coasts and the Americas, war was declared in March 1665. As part of the preparation for war, in February 1665 contracts were signed in Plymouth for digging the ditch and stonework to form the basis of three bastions of a five-bastion citadel on Plymouth Hoe to the west of the Fort, the beginning of a fortress which became the Royal Citadel.

Charles II's main purpose in building the Citadel was ostensibly because he recognised the strategic importance of Plymouth as a coastal town when it came to war on England's enemies. A belief persisted for many years that he had taken ill its unfriendly attitude towards his father and therefore sought some kind of revenge, or at least wished to 'overawe' the town as well as foes across the Channel, though there is little evidence to support this view. The only argument to advance such an idea is a passage from the writings of Cosmo de Medici III, Grand Duke of Tuscany, who visited the King's court in 1669 and visited Plymouth the same year. In it he referred to the Citadel 'which the King built to be a check on the inhabitants who showed themselves on a former occasion to be open to sedition.'

Whatever his reasons, the King requisitioned the land on which it was built, as well as some adjoining land and houses. The formal purchase of the land only began in 1668, though payment was not surprisingly slow to materialise. At the time of building the Citadel, there was no discernible protest by the town at the conveyance of such a substantial area of land to the Crown, perhaps because nobody wished to antagonise the King. A small fort which had been begun after the Spanish Armada but never completed was largely demolished, as was the nearby Chapel of St Catherine, and the military authorities had thus laid claim to all the lands on the Hoe.

The castle had been demolished in the previous autumn, with the lead, timber and stones taken up to the site, and some granite was obtained from Dartmoor. A commission for building the Citadel was dated 17 November 1665, and construction began the following year. It was designed by Sir Bernard de Gomme, the King's Engineer General, with Captain Philip Lanyon in charge of the work under the Lieutenant-Governor, Sir John Skelton. Cannon were set both facing out to sea and into the town, a reminder to residents not to oppose the Crown. Gomme laid the foundation stone on 18 July 1666. Its major architectural feature is the entrance gateway of Portland stone, dated 1670, although the building was not completed for another five years. Once it was finished it also comprised a guard house, governor's house, storehouse, chapel and officers' mess. For some years it also included a statue of Charles II, inscribed 'Carolus Secundus Dei Gratiae Magnae Britanniae Franciae at Hiberniae Rex' (which translates as: Charles II by Grace of God, King of Great Britain, France and Ireland), a reminder that British sovereigns did not formally relinquish the style of King of France until the Act of Union in 1801.

The King paid several visits during construction, and his brother James, Duke of York, accompanied him in July 1671. They stayed in the Citadel itself, inspecting the Cattewater

Southside Street, the Barbican.

and the Hamoaze by day. King Charles was presented with a purse of gold by the mayor, and before leaving the town, according to the contemporary local diarist William Allen 'he touched for the evil [the King's Evil, a scrofulous disease] about 18 persons.'

In September 1681 a party of refugees reached Plymouth from La Rochelle in an open boat. This was a party of French Protestants driven out of the country by the persecution of King Louis XIV, and room was found for them at Stonehouse. Other similar groups followed and two large congregations developed, one at Stonehouse which shared the use of St George's Chapel with the English, the other at Plymouth where their first place of worship was the old friary of the Blackfriars in Southside Street.

As ever, the Crown was always in need of further revenue, and there was regular commandeering of both money and food. In 1684 King Charles called for the surrender of the Great Charter of Queen Elizabeth, and used Lord Chief Justice Jeffreys as his agent, an action which reduced the Corporation's power and numbers. When the council went to attend the surrender at Windsor, they secured the property of the Corporation by transferring it to trustees. When the Charter came back, all its members found themselves dismissed. This new Charter provided for a new mayor, twelve new aldermen, and twelve new councillors (instead of twenty-four), all to serve for life. On his accession in 1685, King James II restored the Corporation to its original form and powers. Though the gesture was welcomed, it was not long before his dogmatic Roman Catholicism alienated him from his people.

When William, Prince of Orange, landed at Brixham in 1688, Plymouth welcomed his fleet into the Sound. It was the first town in England to declare him King, the Citadel was the first fortress handed over to him and a ship, in harbour at the time, was the first English warship to fly his flag. William's declaration was read from the Bench of the Jacobean Guildhall by the mayor. As Plymouth had been no ally of Charles I, and had little reason to be unflinchingly loyal to his sons, perhaps it was not surprising that it should extend a cordial welcome to the man who was coming to rescue England from the increasing tyranny of James II, the second son who was about to lose the throne.

Nevertheless Jacobite sympathies were alive and well in Plymouth, and William's welcome was by no means unanimous. The garrison was unenthusiastic about accepting the new order. Lord Lansdown succeeded his father as governor in 1689, and took no steps to quell a disturbance between town and garrison. The 7th Earl of Huntingdon had been a devoted adherent of James II. When he heard in November 1688 of the arrival of the Dutch fleet under the Prince of Orange, he headed to Plymouth with his regiment, hoping he would be able to hold the Citadel for James II. Instead he 'and the papists' were charged with trying to poison John Grenville, Earl of Bath, the governor of Plymouth, and he was sent to the Tower of London. He was released on 26 December, having been told that his wife had died in childbirth two days earlier.

Bath had been ordered to prepare for the Prince of Orange's invasion, but was one of many members of the nobility whose loyalties to James II had been strained and had been in touch with the Prince through an intermediary. When the invasion came on 5 November 1688 Bath replied that Exeter was impossible to defend, that he thought the militia would prove unreliable, and therefore he would not attempt to assemble it. Even so, well into 1690, declarations in favour of a restoration of James II were being posted up in Plymouth. Bath remained as commander of the regiment and governor of Plymouth until he was asked to retire in 1694.

By this time local industry was still based mainly around the sea and ships, and processing local commodities. A weekly yarn market had existed for some time in the churchyard of St Andrew's Church, and was replaced in 1653 by a proper yarn market built in Old Town. In 1658 a new meat market was built in the middle of Old Town Street with a leather hall above it, leather being an important industry in Plymouth. So too was brewing, and Captain Henry Hatsell, who oversaw work at the naval base, once said impatiently that he wished all the local brewers could be shipped to the West Indies, as their beer produced so much drunkenness in the town.

Towards the late seventeenth century trade developed with the colonies in the West Indies and North America. Sugar and tobacco were imported into Plymouth, while wool and manufactured goods were exported. There was still a coastal trade, with coal from other parts of Britain being brought to Plymouth by sea. Although the commercial port of Plymouth was still growing at the end of the century, it was beginning to lose ground to other ports, its dependence on manufactured imports declining, particularly from north-west Europe. In 1716 it was ranked fourth behind London, Bristol and Exeter. Bristol and Liverpool were building new docks and expanding their trade at this time, but nevertheless foreign trade from Plymouth was still growing. Local goods for export were limited to some woollen goods, lead, tin, copper and building stones. The main import was coal and there was a thriving coastal trade in foodstuffs and household requirements from London.

Although the commercial port may have been slowly but surely declining in national importance behind its rivals, it succeeded in establishing and maintaining a considerable commercial sector independent of the dockyard. In 1700 England was still predominantly an agricultural country, though about a third of national product came from commerce and industry.

During the reign of William III Plymouth began to develop the major industry which would account for much of its prosperity for the next three centuries. Plymouth had been a naval station since the Hundred Years' War with France, and had proved its worth as an important site for the assembly and provisioning of the national fleet, but never had good facilities for repairing men-o'-war as it lacked its own naval yard. Shipbuilding and repairing had therefore been undertaken by several small private concerns operating on the shores of the Cattewater and at Saltash, such as the small ship repair base and ropewalk at Teats Hill, Cattedown. Refitting was also carried out from a hulk established in the Cattewater by Cromwell. In 1663 the navy board ordered the sale of the hulk and the construction of shipyards, but the yards were never built. Towards the end of the Elizabethan era, Sir Walter Raleigh had proposed that Hamoaze should be developed as a naval harbour, and later Saltash was suggested as a likely base. These ideas came to nothing, mainly because fishermen and other local people objected on the grounds that a naval yard would either ruin their trade or else spoil their gardens and views. At this time England's royal shipyards were concentrated around the Thames and Medway estuaries and at Portsmouth. The need for another yard further west was underlined by the Dutch raid on the River Medway in 1667 and the ever-present threat of war with France. Alternative sites such as Milford Haven, Falmouth, Dartmouth and Bideford were suggested, but the naval authorities eventually chose Plymouth.

In view of the recent naval action against Holland, it was ironic that the accession of a Dutch Prince to the British throne should set in motion the realisation of this scheme. In 1689 plans were drawn up for a dockyard at Devonport, and in December 1690 a contract was signed for clearing the site on which the original dockyard was about to be built. King William came to inspect it, Parliament voted about £2 million for the project, and in September 1691 construction work began on the first dock to the west, on the banks of the Hamoaze. The site, two miles from Plymouth, partly on the Mount Wise estate, was separated from the town by marshes near the site of present-day Union Street. As the naval yards were not part of Plymouth, for some years access was easiest by sea. The first docks were completed in 1693, to be supplemented within the next few years by a row of officers' houses on a terrace overlooking the docks, a storehouse, and a ropehouse.

As the dockyard expanded through the eighteenth century, so did the surrounding township, which came to be known initially as Plymouth Dock and later as Devonport. Initially it was comprised of people from neighbouring towns and villages, as there were no houses for the workers at first. In the early years, some had to be lodged on ships anchored in the Hamoaze. A barrier to the provision of further housing was the refusal until 1700 of the Morice trustees to part with any of their land for housing. Once land was released, houses were built parallel with the north dockyard wall at North Corner, later called Cornwall Street. By 1712 there were 318 men employed and by 1733 Plymouth Dock had 3,000 people.

At the end of the seventeenth century the first of Plymouth's lighthouses was built, on the Eddystone Rocks, a few miles off the south coast. This first lighthouse was an octagonal wooden structure built by Henry Winstanley, a former mercer in the City of London. After he had lost two ships on the Eddystone, he decided that a light to mark the treacherous area was needed. Construction started in 1696 and the edifice was first lit on 14 November 1698. While it was still under construction, a French privateer took Winstanley prisoner but King Louis XIV of France immediately gave orders for his

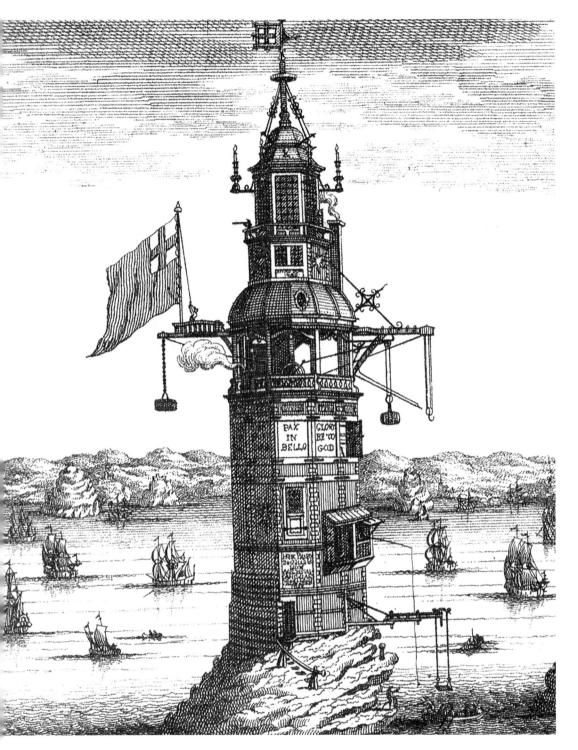

Henry Winstanley's Lighthouse, built in 1696 and destroyed by a storm in 1703.

Stoke Damerel Church.

release, saying that France was at war with England, not with humanity. Though the lighthouse survived its first winter, next year it was found to be badly in need of repair, so the structure was removed and replaced. It lasted in its modified state until destroyed by a great storm on the night of 26 November 1703. Winstanley and some workmen were on the lighthouse to complete some additions to the structure when they were all washed away to sea. The second construction, a round, smooth wooden tower, was built by John Rudyard in 1708, and lit for the first time a year later. It lasted over forty years until it burnt down in 1755.

Stoke Damerel was initially the parish church for Plymouth Dock, although almost a mile away from the new town. It was enlarged several times in the eighteenth century, beginning with a new north aisle added in about 1730. Parish registers for the church over the period 1690–1715 showed that over half the extra-parochial people married there were from Plymouth and neighbouring parts of Devon and Cornwall, as well as from other English naval ports such as Portsmouth and Chatham, and even further afield.

The 'old' Plymouth viewed the birth and growth of this competitive township with some suspicion. Large numbers of tradespeople and workmen were moving to the dock, which had grown from nothing to half the population of Plymouth in less than fifty years and looked set to overtake it before much longer.

five

Georgian Plymouth

The conflicts of the eighteenth century, particularly the War of the Austrian Succession of 1741–8 and the Seven Years' War of 1756–63, provided additional trade and employment for Plymouth and Plymouth Dock. Both townships, and the smaller but nevertheless growing Stonehouse, were expanding, with the inevitable consequences of overcrowding, lack of housing and unsanitary conditions.

The commercial port of Plymouth was the centre of healthy business, with the town quay dues which had doubled between 1670 and 1700 and had doubled again by 1720. In terms of tonnage and ships engaged in trade between 1715 and 1717, Plymouth ranked fourth among English ports. Exports from the Plymouth hinterland were limited; there were woollens overseas, some lead, tin and copper from Dartmoor to South Wales, paving stones and slates, some of which went to the American colonies. During the eighteenth century coal imports from Newcastle fell steadily, to be replaced by supplies from South Wales and from Whitehaven. The coasting imports consisted mainly of corn, groceries and other foodstuffs, as well as household goods from London and other sources which supplied Plymouth and were re-shipped in smaller craft to West Country ports between Exeter and St Ives.

Between 1722 and 1731 Plymouth imported direct almost 3,000,000lb of tobacco, most of which was re-exported. As the duties mounted on tobacco, direct imports moved increasingly to Bristol and Liverpool, where the richer merchants could find the capital required. The sugar crop was also drawn off to these ports. In 1750 Plymouth built its first sugar house for grinding cane, near the western end of the modern Mount Gould Road, when Bristol alone already had sixteen. Yet foreign trade was growing in Plymouth at this time. In 1750 there were sixteen ships in the West Indies, and another twelve sailing to the mainland American colonies.

Among famous visitors to Plymouth at the time was the writer Daniel Defoe, who published his impressions in *Journey from London to Land's End* in 1724. The town, he noted, was …

> … indeed a town of consideration and of great importance to the public, nor is the trade carried on here inconsiderable. The town is populous and wealthy. As for gentlemen, it cannot be expected to find many such in a town depending on trade and shipping; yet I found here some men of value whose society obliges me to say that a gentleman might find very agreeable company in Plymouth.

Plymouth Dock, *c.* 1780.

Less enthusiastic was the physician and antiquary William Maton, visiting some seven decades later. In his *Observations on the Western Counties of England*, published 1794–6, he called Plymouth 'an ill-built, disagreeable place, infested with all the filthiness so frequent in seaports.' As for Plymouth Dock, he wrote that 'from the bustle and continual passing of people we would fancy ourselves in the outskirts of London.'

The wall that had protected Plymouth during the siege fell into disuse and was obstructing expansion. It was looted steadily for new building projects, and by mid-century the gates within the wall had become redundant. Most of the gates were gradually demolished, Friary Gate in 1763, Gascoigne (North) Gate in 1768, and Frankfort (West) Gate in 1783. The narrowness of the gates, from the days of pure horse travel, had in fact become an inconvenience to the new wagons travelling in and out of the town.

In 1753 an Act was passed which allowed turnpikes, privately owned and requiring payment of a toll for use, as far west as Exeter. A turnpike road from Plymouth to London was completed in 1758, while other new roads in the area were built and existing ones improved. In 1767 an Act was passed which empowered Lord Mount Edgcumbe and Sir John St Aubyn to build a bridge over Stonehouse Creek. Because of the cost of construction, they were given the right to collect tolls afterwards. The bridge was built in 1773, with pedestrians being charged a halfpenny to cross, hence its popular name 'Ha'penny Bridge'. A ferry to Torpoint began operating in 1791. On the east side of Plymouth, Lord Boringdon reclaimed some of the Plympton marshes to build a road to his house at Saltram, promoted the Plymouth Embankment Co. which drained the marshes at Laira, and enabled the building of the new Embankment Road from Crabtree to Plymouth. The next link in the new route between Breton Side and Embankment Road was opened in 1810.

Carriages began to operate in about 1775, running regular services from Old Town to Fore Street, Plymouth Dock, for a fare of 1s. Sedan chairs were in use, costing 6d for short journeys. Hackney coaches and chaises were also available. In 1796 William Birch of Stoke Damerel introduced a coach service from Plymouth to Exeter. A Board of Commissioners was set up to pave the streets, light the town, and install drains, and to make Plymouth more attractive, elm trees were planted around Millbay, Pennycomequick, Frankfort Gate and the Hoe.

Plymouth's second lighthouse, built by John Rudyard, was destroyed by fire on 2 December 1755. Three keepers battled to save it, but in vain; they were driven outside the building to shelter in the rocks, and were rescued by fishermen from Cawsand. One of the keepers, aged ninety-four, said that as he was looking up through the tower some molten lead ran down his throat. He died twelve days later, and a post-mortem examination revealed a piece of lead weighing 7oz in his stomach. In December 1756 John Smeaton and a team of masons began work on a third lighthouse. Six months later the first course of interlocking Portland stone blocks was laid, and construction was completed in August 1759.

The synagogue in Catherine Street, built in 1762 after Hebrew families settled in Broad Hoe Lane from about 1740 onwards, is the oldest Ashkenazi synagogue (for those of central European origin) remaining in the English-speaking world.

Theatre in the town could be traced back to about 1515 when a troupe of strolling players, the King's Joculars, appeared at the town gates to come and entertain. They presumably had a good reception, as from then onwards several companies of players arrived at the town several times a year. Not everybody enjoyed their visits; some pious local dignitaries thought the gates should be slammed shut in the faces of these itinerant actors, while others suggested paying them to go away and take their activities elsewhere. Some groups were sponsored by the nobility and bore the name of their sponsor, among them Lord Dudley's Players, who played in Plymouth in the 1560s, giving performances in the open air or in venues such as St Andrew's Church.

With the advent of the Puritan age and the Civil War, such performances were even more *persona non grata*, and Plymouth had to wait until 1745 for its first theatre. This was built in two rooms in a dilapidated house in Broad Hoe Lane, later Hoegate Street, with seating for about 100 people. Audiences and players alike became known for their riotous behaviour, and the structure of the building became so unsafe that it was abandoned in 1758. It was replaced by a more robust building at the top of the newly developing George Street, which called itself the Theatre Royal after being honoured by a visit from King George III and various members of his family in the summer of 1789. With him were Queen Charlotte and their three eldest daughters the Princesses Charlotte, the Princess Royal, Augusta, and Elizabeth. They stayed at Saltram House (where their host was Lord Boringdon), visited Mount Edgcumbe and Cotehele, and the King also reviewed about a hundred ships in Plymouth Sound.

This was one of several royal visits to Plymouth at around this time. Prince William, the King's third son, who had joined the Royal Navy, made various appearances in Plymouth. In March 1786 he was initiated as a Freemason at the Prince George Inn, Vauxhall Street, and later that year he was given the Freedom of Plymouth. After naval service in the Americas he returned to Plymouth, and lodged for a while at a merchant's house. In 1788 his two elder brothers, the Prince of Wales and Frederick,

Duke of York, came to Plymouth to see him, paying duty visits to the Citadel, the dockyard, and Mount Edgcumbe, when not sampling the best high life that the town had to offer, or as contemporaries eloquently said, 'painting the town red.'

Several famous schools were established at Plymouth in the seventeenth and eighteenth centuries. They included the Grey Coat School, the Household of Faith and Lady Rogers' School. Plympton Grammar School was completed in 1671. After a meeting held at Plymouth Guildhall in 1809, a public school was planned, resulting in a boys' school being opened near the Pig Market in Bedford Street. It moved to Cobourg Street in 1812 and was joined by a girls' school. Schools were also established in St John Street, Plymouth Dock, about 1799, Stoke Public School in 1809 and schools in Stonehouse, in Quarry Street and Union Lane.

In the eighteenth century, the headmaster of Plympton Grammar School was Samuel Reynolds. His son Joshua was to become the institution's most famous pupil, a renowned portrait painter and founding President of the Royal Academy of Arts in 1768. Reynolds bought his friend Dr Samuel Johnson on a visit to Plymouth in 1762, and the latter noticed that Plymouth seemed somewhat 'stirred by jealousy' of the new community at Dock. When he was told that Plymouth had a plentiful supply of water from reservoirs but Dock had none (obviously excluding sea water) but needed some, according to his diarist Boswell, he 'was violent in opposition, and half laughing at himself for his pretended zeal,' declared, 'No, no! I am against the Dockers. I am a Plymouth man. Rogues! Let them die of thirst, they shall not have a drop.'

Other great names from the golden age of British painting were born in Plymouth during the latter years of the eighteenth century. Foremost amongst them were James Northcote, who specialised in grand historical scenes as well as portraits, Samuel Prout, best remembered for his landscape watercolour paintings and drawings, and the ambitious but ill-fated historical artist Benjamin Robert Haydon, whose career was destined to end in failure, poverty and death by his own hand.

As if to show that the spirit of the age of Queen Elizabeth was not a thing of the past, three historic expeditions left Plymouth during this time. Captain Cook sailed from Plymouth on all his voyages. In 1768 he left in the *Endeavour* to sail round the world and in 1772 he sailed for New Zealand in the *Resolution*. Captain Furneaux of Swilly was in the ship *Adventure* which accompanied Cook on the latter voyage. His second voyage in the *Resolution*, which left in 1776, nearly did not start at all as the ships were almost wrecked under the Citadel. It was one of many shipwrecks and similar incidents which suggested the need for a breakwater to provide shelter in Plymouth Sound.

The major expansion of the dockyard came in the late eighteenth and early nineteenth centuries during war with France. With brief intervals, Britain and France, or French allies, were at war for much of the period from 1738 to 1815. The theatre of war was generally the Atlantic, the Mediterranean and the West Indies, and Plymouth was the most strategically placed naval base. The town therefore prospered, and when the Seven Years' War broke out in 1756 Captain George Rodney was the senior officer present. That spring he was in charge of the dockyard and the ships' companies. There was a widespread fear of invasion and the defence lines around Plymouth Dock, from the high ground south of the road to Torpoint Ferry to Stonehouse Creek, were begun. Behind the lines half a dozen squares of small barracks were built, and in 1757 'the best wages in the country' were being advertised as far away as Sherborne for forty masons and bricklayers to build barracks at Dock. By 1759 over £25,000 had been spent on local defences.

The dockyard workers who walked to work each day wanted to live close to the dock. In the eighteenth century new houses were built nearby and the new town gradually developed. By the mid-eighteenth century it had a population of about 4,000.

Some additional land was bought at Stonehouse at the outbreak of war for a naval hospital; more land was later bought from Lord Edgcumbe and building began in 1758 on the shores of Stonehouse Creek. It has been suggested that the catalyst for provision of such an institution was as a result of the sinking of HMS *Ramillies* near Salcombe in February 1760, about nine days after leaving Plymouth, with a loss of some 700 sailors, but records show that the hospital was already partly built by this time. The first patients were transferred from the old hospital near Derry's Clock later in 1760, and when the hospital was completed in 1762 it was the first in England built in small blocks, enabling groups of patients to be isolated from one another. As there were landing steps down to the water's edge, sick and wounded seamen could be landed directly from boats. Later a military hospital was built on the opposite shore of the creek. In 1773 the Edgcumbe family leased land for the development of Durnford Street and Emma Place as a suburb comprising elegant neo-classical town houses, most of which were soon acquired by the families of naval officers.

At around the same time the dockyard itself was being expanded to the south. The original ropehouse which had formed the southern boundary of the yard was demolished, and another ropehouse was built on a north-south line. A mast pond, new store, mast and boat houses were established, as well as two building slips on the site of the present slips. A new road was built to Mutton Cove, the little basin still at the southern boundary of the dockyard. On the other side of the yard a third dry dock, the North Dock, was added in 1762, with more building slips. Improvements to the yard continued for another ten years or so, with a total expenditure of around £153,000. Much of this work continued during the uncertain peace years of 1763 and 1776, when the navy suffered from political neglect.

During the wars, spies and infiltrators were busy at work. From 1776 the American War of Independence brought back more dockyard work for defence purposes. There were sabotage attempts in the dockyard when French, Spanish and American agents tried to gain some advantage. One spy, Comte de Parades, who claimed to be the descendant of a Spanish Count though he was probably the son of a humble French pastry-cook with a good knowledge of languages, well-informed on naval affairs and above all an accomplished liar, came to visit English ports and dockyards and look for agents. In his memoirs he later claimed that he successfully induced somebody in the English Ministry to send him copies of all Admiralty Orders. Next he managed, probably by bribing a sergeant on duty, to obtain plans and make sketches of the dockyard and Citadel, which he passed to his masters in France. This led to an assault on Plymouth by a combined Franco-Spanish fleet of sixty ships and 30,000 men, which arrived off the Sound and anchored in Cawsand Bay on 6 August 1779 and made the authorities realise there was need for action. Old cannon were dragged out and placed in prominent positions, a boom was placed across the Cattewater and prisoners of war were dispersed around the area in order that they would not escape and join 'the enemy.' A storm on 21 August drove the ships into the open water and in sight of Sir Charles Hardy, who was cruising in the Channel with a small group of naval ships. Although superior in numbers, the French fleet backed away from a confrontation and sailed back home without a shot being fired. It was the only serious threat of invasion faced by Plymouth since the Breton raids of the fifteenth century. Parades was charged with treachery and served fourteen months in the Bastille before being released.

Plans were quickly made to build new gun batteries around the Sound, as well as a blockhouse at Higher Stoke. After the Royal Marines force was raised in 1755 the Plymouth Division was billeted around Sutton Harbour with an orderly room in Southside Street, a limestone-faced building between Southside Ope and Parade Ope. Work on building new barracks started in 1781 on land bought from Lord Edgcumbe, a long block for the men running along the western water's edge of Millbay with the officers' quarters at right angles at the two ends. It was first occupied in 1783 and completed within another two years. By then Stonehouse ranked as an attractive town with a population of almost 4,000.

In 1789 work began on the fourth dry dock, the New North Dock. When King George III and Queen Charlotte visited it while under construction, he asked why the dock was being built on a larger scale than the original design had provided for. He was told that the French were building a new ship, *Commerce de Marseilles*, which was even longer than the design length of the dock, and therefore it had to be made long enough to accommodate such enemy vessels. In fact the ship was captured at Toulon shortly after the outbreak of war in 1793 and was thus the first ship to enter the new dock. The royal family also visited the Citadel and the Victualling Office. The most spectacular event of their visit was a review of the fleet and mock naval battle in the Sound, with about a hundred ships taking part.

Preparations for war had been made sometime beforehand. Under the authority of the Duke of Richmond, Master-General of the Ordinance, a second wall was built around Dock, behind the main line with its barracks and the civilian houses. He moved the seat of the Governor of Plymouth from the Citadel to a new house at Mount Wise, built as Government House in 1820 as the private residence and military offices of the Lieutenant-Governor of the Plymouth Garrison. Prior to 1725 the Governor's offices had been at the Royal Citadel. In 1935 it was taken over by the Admiralty and, under its new name of Admiralty House, became the new offices of the Commander-in-Chief at Devonport.

When war broke out in 1793 Plymouth was full of troops, some being accommodated during the summer in camps at Roborough and Maker. Plymouth featured prominently in the ensuing conflict. In May 1794 Earl Howe, in command of the Channel Fleet, left the Sound to attack a French fleet of twenty-six sailing off Brest, resulting in victory in the third battle of Ushant, otherwise known as the 'glorious first of June.' That same year Shepherd's woollen manufactory near Frankfort Place was made into a barracks, and another was built beside the Millbay prisoner of war establishment.

Following extensive military campaigns in the West Indies, Plymouth was flooded with sick and wounded soldiers in 1795, and many died. A temporary and very inadequate hospital at the friary proved insufficient for the town's needs, and the Naval Hospital did not admit soldiers. As a result the Military Hospital was built in 1797 on the northern shores of Stonehouse Creek facing the Naval Hospital, following a similar pattern of small blocks, in this case four, linked by a large colonnade.

Vice-Admiral Nelson was also seen in Plymouth during the Napoleonic wars. In January 1801 he hoisted his flag on board the *San Josef* in Plymouth Sound in the Channel Fleet under the command of the Earl St Vincent. A few days later he was offered and accepted the Freedom of the City of Plymouth, having had a similar invitation from Exeter the day before.

War was formally declared on France in May 1803 with an announcement by the Commander-in-Chief, Admiral Dacres. He was well aware that public proclamation of such news would lead to a mass exodus from the town of men intent on avoiding being called up to serve their country, so he took the precaution beforehand of confining troops to barracks, ordering closure of and guards on the town gates, and sending Marines to patrol the streets. Next press gangs were set to work recruiting for the navy at inns, theatres and private houses in Plymouth and in the neighbouring villages. Even fishermen at sea were likely to be tackled, and in one day alone forty trawlers off the Eddystone were deprived of two-thirds of their crews.

Large numbers of prisoners were captured during the French and American wars, and the numbers brought to Plymouth greatly exceeded the capacity of the prison at Millbay. In 1762 there were 7,000 housed at Millbay and elsewhere. The prison was overcrowded and unsanitary, the quality of the food was poor, and there were frequent escapes, the most notable being when 150 gained their freedom by digging a tunnel. Hulks were moored in the Hamoaze for the overspill, but the situation was not remedied properly until 1805 when Sir Thomas Tyrwhitt, Member of Parliament for Plymouth, proposed building a new prison at the newly-founded Princetown on Dartmoor at an eventual cost of £200,000. The first 5,000 prisoners were transferred there in 1809, and by 1813 it held 1,700 American prisoners and 8,000 French prisoners. The end of the war with France in 1815 resulted in a reduction in the number of inmates, but proved a mixed blessing for Plymouth as it meant less work and many men were laid off from the dockyard.

The prison, Princetown. (Courtesy of M. Richards)

During the years of fighting there were the usual unsavoury incidents associated with times of war, such as press gangs at loose, food shortages and rising prices. Mobs pillaged shops and attacked tradesmen, and on one occasion a riot was only averted when the government agreed that army and naval supplies could be sold to the general public. The naval mutiny which started at Spithead in 1797 quickly spread to other ports. In Plymouth and the dockyard, the Red Flag flew from every masthead, but the authorities had been well prepared. Officials at Plymouth told the men that the Admiralty had just decided to increase pay by 1s a day, and asked the officers to refrain from arresting the ringleaders. When news came a day later from Portsmouth that the Admiralty had gone back on this promise, made arrests and fired on those whom they thought were the ringleaders, the trouble escalated. Officers were turned off their ships, some were thrown into the harbour, and mobs rampaged through the three towns, breaking into the private houses of the authorities and creating panic among the civilians. The mutiny was only quelled when Admiral Viscount Keith, who had helped to restore order at the main insurrection at the Nore, addressed the men in person from the deck of the *Saturn*. He admonished them for encouraging the country's enemies and called for the instant surrender of fifty sailors, whose names he held in his hand, as a condition of pardon for the rest. When men with bayonets at the ready threatened him, he calmly drew his sword and said he would run it through the first to come near him. His authority prevailed, and of those who surrendered fourteen were condemned to death for their part in the mutiny at Dock, while many more were sentenced to the cat o'nine tails.

A plot was discovered among the Royal Marines by a drummer boy who overheard an oath being administered to a private, vowing to help in any uprising which might take place. When the boy reported it, the Commandant at once ordered the closing of the barrack gates, mustered the whole division and had it disarmed. It remained without arms until the conspiracy had been completely unearthed. The three ringleaders, an Englishman and two Irishmen, had held secret meetings to organise a rising 'to release the French prisoners, and not to rest till they had overturned the Government.' They were condemned to death by court martial, and were taken to the Hoe in a procession following their own coffins, on which they knelt while a firing squad shot them in the presence of the assembled troops and people of the towns, no doubt as an example to others.

Other unpleasant occurrences were recorded at around this time. In 1787 two men in the dockyard, John Richards, a ropemaker, and William Smith, a tailor, had had a grievance against Philip Smith, a clerk. They were condemned to death for murder, hanged at Heavitree, near Exeter, and their bodies were brought back to near the scene of their crime. They were suspended from a gibbet on the beach of the Deadlake, near Stoke Damerel Church. In 1830 the same area became a magnet for bodysnatchers, who found the churchyard provided rich pickings for stealing bodies and selling them for anatomical research. Eventually the main people responsible were apprehended and transported.

When news of the victory at the Battle of Trafalgar in October 1805 reached Plymouth, an actor ran on to the stage in the theatre and interrupted the play to bring the audience the glad tidings. There was an outburst of cheering, until he raised his hand and went on to announce the death of Nelson, after which many tears were shed in public. Nevertheless, victory seemed to remove any immediate threat of French invasion, though it was not the end of the war. The activities of stray French warships and the depredations of privateers in the Channel prompted the completion of all the ships on which construction had started. When the Peninsular War against France broke out in 1807, Plymouth was full of transports crowded with reinforcements for the army, but they did not sail, and other ships bound for the Peninsula from Portsmouth were diverted into Plymouth to await orders.

In January 1809 ships came into the Sound bringing the remnants of the army defeated at Corunna, with 800 women who had followed their husbands to Spain and lived through an inferno following the retreat. Many were dying of starvation and or exhaustion and wounds, with hundreds of officers and soldiers maimed. Many died before they could be landed. Hospitals could not hold all the survivors who needed treatment, even after the ships in the Hamoaze had been filled. People throughout the town gave up their bedrooms to accommodate them, and the mayor called a public meeting to organise relief for the soldiers' wives and families who were landing from Spain. Very soon £1,800 had been raised, the women contributed clothing for the refugees and the town volunteers gave their uniforms to destitute soldiers.

In April 1809 Sir Arthur Wellesley (who became the Duke of Wellington in 1814) was at Plymouth to inspect the army with which he would begin his Peninsular campaign and to take a ship from Lisbon with the first contingent. The port was busy with embarking reinforcements, stores, guns and ammunition. Throughout the campaign Plymouth was fully engaged in handling the huge military traffic to Portugal and supplying the naval guard on the Channel and the Bay of Biscay. In 1812 Wellesley embarked from Plymouth on his way to a victorious battle at Salamanca.

At least Plymouth escaped any direct involvement in the war of 1812 with the United States of America. There was nevertheless an interesting local connection after a battle in the English Channel between HMS *Pelican* and the American brig *Argus*. The American captain, William Allen, was severely wounded, the midshipman, Richard Delphey, was killed outright, and both were brought ashore at the town. Allen's leg was amputated, but it failed to save his life. He had been known in Plymouth as a humane officer, always kind to British prisoners in his hands. Both men were buried with signal marks of respect and regret in St Andrew's Church, at a ceremony in which 500 Red Marines with their band headed the procession from the hospital to the church, and British and American naval officers walked together behind the coffins. A memorial stone to them was raised between St Andrew's and the Prysten House.

While the dockyard dominated industry in Plymouth in the eighteenth century, there was also a considerable trade in weaving. The Shepherd family had factories close to the quay near Coxside, and mills at Buckfastleigh, Ashburton, Tavistock and Totnes. William Shepherd gave one-tenth of his profits to be divided among the poor. William Cookworthy, the father of English porcelain, set up the first factory for his wares in 1766 and received a patent for his wares in 1768. He stored his porcelain in a warehouse built in about 1650 on the edge of Sutton Harbour, a building which remains the oldest surviving water's-edge warehouse in Britain. Declining profits forced him to move his business from Plymouth to Bristol in 1774. Other major industries in the town at this time included leather and brewing, in addition to the long–established and still successful trade in fishing. The need for more new streets and housing continued to provide employment on a wide scale. Plymouth remained a major port, trading with the West Indies, the American colonies and Mediterranean countries. There was also much coastal trade, with grain and coal brought by sea from other parts of Britain into Plymouth and tin being exported.

Black Friars Distillery, Southside Street, the oldest working gin
distillery in England. (© M. Richards)

Plymouth has been synonymous with gin ever since the Coates family acquired
the former Black Friars monastery in Southside Street in 1793. They perfected the
making of dry gin by using crystal clear Dartmoor water, and Plymouth gin was
soon adopted by naval officers as their favourite drink. Plymouth Original Strength,
41.2 per cent alcohol by volume, has a distinctively different, sweeter flavour from the
more commonly available London Dry Gin. A navy strength variety is also available,
57 per cent alcohol by volume, the traditional strength demanded by the Royal Navy
as this was the proof that would not prevent gunpowder from igniting, should it
be compromised by spilled spirit. Since 1945 the firm has been owned by various
international companies, but in 1996 it was bought by Plymouth men who changed
the name of the firm back to Coates.

Business life was helped by the foundation of banks in the town. John Baring of
Exeter, one of the original Baring Brothers who founded the firm in London bearing

their name, launched the first bank in Plymouth in 1772, known initially as Baring, Lee, Sellons & Tingcombe, and later as the Plymouth Bank. A year later came Harris, Harris, Tanner & Herbert, which would become the Naval Bank. Plymouth Dock's first bank was founded in 1788 by Elford, Elford & Hartwell. Most of these were local institutions based on the capital of the partners rather than the great national institutions of later years. Partners changed over the years, and both towns could boast several more private banks by 1800. By making credit available, and issuing bank notes, they facilitated business life considerably. In 1818 Thomas Gill started an alkali and soap factory at Millbay. This was the first of several important trades carried on there, as a glass factory was built nearby, and in 1823 the United Gas Factory was established. These all helped to establish Millbay as the main factory area of Plymouth. In 1813 the Port of Plymouth Chamber of Commerce was founded, one of the oldest in the country.

After the Battle of Waterloo in June 1815 Napoleon Bonaparte was captured on board HMS *Bellerophon*, brought to Torbay and then Plymouth, and the ship remained in Plymouth Sound for two weeks before he was exiled to St Helena. While on the ship, he seemed gratified by the interest shown in him, and he was content to walk on deck and stand in the gangway in full public view. Recalling the appearance of King Jean in 1357, no other English town could boast that it had twice seen, or played host to, a captive ruler of France. *Bellerophon* was renamed *Captivity* and returned to use as a convict ship before being broken up in 1832. Some of the ship's timber was used by Dr George Bellamy, who had been the surgeon on board, for part of a new cottage he was building at Plymstock. A further local Bonaparte connection came when Plymouth-born artist Charles Lock Eastlake, who later followed in the footsteps of Sir Joshua Reynolds and became a President of the Royal Academy, made sketches of the former Emperor with his full approval. His sitter even posed in the gangway for him, and sent ashore for some parts of his uniform in order to ensure that the picture would be accurate in as much detail as possible. Eastlake used his work to paint an imposing picture of the captive former Emperor on the deck of the ship, a work which made him famous at the age of twenty-two.

Victories at the Battles of Trafalgar and Waterloo had made Britain one of the major European powers. The nation owed much of its prestige to sea power, and as the role of the navy expanded over the next century, Plymouth and Devonport were uniquely placed to take advantage of this status and the subsequent growth in maritime industry.

In 1812 construction of the Breakwater in Plymouth Sound was authorised by an Order in Council. It was built almost three miles south of the Hoe to provide a safe haven for ships sheltering from southerly storms. Several great admirals of the time had found Cawsand Bay too dangerous as an anchorage and preferred Torbay, but somewhere safer near Plymouth was required. Lord St Vincent had made the suggestion as early as 1779, when captain of the *Foudroyant*. When he became Commander-in-Chief of the Channel Fleet in 1806 he asked the Admiralty to consider various remedies, of which the Breakwater was eventually chosen. He resigned a year later and the idea was temporarily put aside, but it was taken up again in 1811 and the Admiralty agreed to adopt the plans made in 1806. The first stone was laid in 1812, from limestone purchased from the Duke of Bedford at the Oreston quarries. As the stone was quarried, trains of trucks took it away to the wharves where they were to run on vessels provided with rails and tipping devices, and they discharged their cargoes overboard at the site. The process was undertaken so quickly that, had it not been for errors in underestimating the force of the sea, the Breakwater would have been completed in

Sir Joshua Reynolds, the
Plympton-born painter
and first President of the
Royal Academy of Arts.

Oreston, *c.* 1820.

much less time. A great storm in 1817 shifted hundreds of thousands of tons of rock and altered the angle, but the engineers continued undaunted. In another severe storm in 1824, when twenty-five ships were driven ashore in the Sound, sea damage altered the angle again, and left the designers with another 200,000 tons of stone to replace. Work then went on without any further interruption and it was completed in 1848, at an estimated total cost of £1.5 million. Once it was completed, shipping casualties in the Sound were almost unknown, even in bad weather.

The real source of wealth and the major employer in the region became the dockyard. Plymouth Dock had outgrown its confines sandwiched between the dockyard walls,

The Royal Union Baths, Union Street, 1829. (Courtesy of M. Richards)

The Royal Theatre and Athenaeum, 1832.

and development began at Morice Town behind the Torpoint Ferry landing area on the Devon bank. New villages were also developing at Lower Stoke and Higher Stoke.

In 1801, at the time of the first census, Plymouth had a population of 19,000 and Stonehouse had 3,407. Plymouth Dock had overtaken Plymouth with a population of 23,000, and demanded recognition as an independent entity. By 1821 Dock's figure was 33,578, against that of Plymouth which was 21,591. Dock had already discovered a sense of its own civic pride with the buildings of John Foulston, who had built a Town Hall for Devonport at the top of Ker Street. Completed in 1821, it was financed as a private undertaking by a group of shareholders and consisted of a large hall, which served as a magistrates' court and assembly room. Another of his distinctive buildings was his Egyptian building of 1823, which was originally intended as the Plymouth Dock and Stonehouse Classical and Mathematical School, but became the Civil and Military Library in 1827.

In January 1810 a competition was announced for designs for a tavern, ballroom and theatre in three distinct buildings. The competition was won by John Foulston, who submitted a design bringing all three elements together. The main frontage of the block of buildings, comprising the Royal Hotel, Assembly Rooms and Theatre Royal, facing George Place, was dominated by a portico with 30ft-high Ionic columns, with the theatre lying to the west of the portico and the ballroom and hotel to the east. The hotel contained suites of rooms for between twenty and thirty families, a large dining room, coffee room, commercial room, billiard room and thirteen smaller dining rooms. As a fire precaution, the theatre was separated from the hotel by thick walls. The inner structure was made of cast iron, and Foulston claimed it was the only fireproof theatre in England. The auditorium was capable of accommodating 1,192 people in a three-quarter circle.

Foulston's second public building in Plymouth was the Proprietary Library in Cornwall Street, founded at a meeting held in November 1811 and thus the oldest library in the city. Although known as the Plymouth Public Library, it was privately owned by its subscribers. His next task was to prepare a design for an Exchange which was never adopted. A subsequent major commission, undertaken in 1818, was the Athenaeum for the Plymouth Institution, built in temple-like form to the west of the Theatre Royal. During the next five years he was designing buildings in Devonport, but returned to Plymouth in 1823 to design St Catherine's Chapel, facing the eastern wing of the Royal Hotel.

Also in 1823 Plymouth Dock petitioned King George IV for permission to change its name. This was granted in an order dated 24 December 1823, signed by Sir Robert Peel, then Home Secretary, and on 1 January 1824 the name Devonport was officially used for the first time. As a lasting memorial to the occasion, Foulston's 124ft-high Doric column was erected. It was aligned with Union Street, linking Stonehouse with Plymouth in what the latter could only regard as a somewhat provocative gesture. The official proclamation, carried from point to point in the town, was read over and over again to cheering crowds, houses were decorated, and there was public feasting.

In 1820 the new Customs House was built at Sutton Harbour. The Royal William Victualling Yard at Stonehouse, designed by Sir John Rennie, was built between 1824 and 1835 at a cost of £700,000. It occupied fourteen acres, nearly half of which had been recovered from the sea at Stonehouse Creek. The Duke of Clarence laid the coping stone of the sea wall, and the gateway was later surmounted by a large statue of the Duke, who ascended the throne in 1830 as King William IV. As a monarch who had visited Plymouth on occasion before ascending the throne, the connection was appropriate. His consort Queen Adelaide, while still Duchess of Clarence, had opened Laira Bridge in 1827.

The New Victualling Offices, Devil's Point, 1832.

Sutton Pool and Customs House, 1830. (Courtesy of M. Richards)

Devonport in the early nineteenth century, after a drawing by J.M.W. Turner.

Devonport Town Hall, Column and Egyptian Library, designed by John Foulston.

Devonport built its first steamship, the 813-ton *Rhadamanthus*, in 1831-2, but as local engineering capacity was limited, the vessel had to sail to Woolwich to have its engines fitted. The old South Yard could not furnish the workshops or the kind of dock needed for these ships, and a new steam factory was planned.

In 1827 Devonport lodged a formal request for representation by its own Member of Parliament, and directly petitioned William, Duke of Clarence, on his formal visit to the town in 1828. In the election of 1830 which followed the accession of the Duke as King William IV, reformers swept the county seats in Devon and Cornwall, but the Plymouth boroughs returned two official nominees. Those who demanded reform in Plymouth and Devonport held a mass meeting, after which a petition urging reform was sent to the Plymouth Members.

The first Reform Bill was presented to Parliament in March 1831, and after its defeat there were public protest meetings outside the Royal Hotel in Plymouth and Devonport Town Hall. When another election was held later that year the sitting Members, Admirals Byam Martin and Cockburn, both anti-reform, were returned yet again, and at the close of polling an escort of over a hundred soldiers had to try and protect Cockburn, who had his head cut by a brick in the angry demonstrations. The mayor had to read the Riot Act to the assembled crowds twice before they would disperse. Dr Phillpotts, the Tory Bishop of Exeter, found the spirit in Plymouth most unfavourable, and was asked not to visit Plymouth to consecrate a new church as he would probably be in great personal danger.

Though the new ministry carried the Bill through the Commons in July 1831, it was rejected by the Lords in October. After redrafting it returned to the Lords in the spring of 1832, and news that it had been thrown out again in May resulted in flags throughout Plymouth flying at half-mast, and muffled peals rang out on church bells. Four days later there was a meeting of 26,000 from the Three Towns in the Bull Ring near the Hoe to support the Bill. Its passage in June greatly enlarged the electorate by granting the vote to all men who leased or owned land worth £10 or more, and tenants-at-will paying an annual rent of £50. More than 10,000 people marched the streets in procession under triumphal arches, and another meeting in the Bull Ring was held to celebrate.

Stonehouse and Devonport were joined together as a parliamentary borough as a result of the Great Reform Bill of 1832, thus electing two Members of Parliament. The first Members for Devonport were Sir George Grey, later Home Secretary, and Admiral Sir Edward Codrington, who had commanded a ship in Nelson's fleet at the Battle of Trafalgar and later fought bravely at the Battle at Navarino during the Greek Wars of Independence in 1827.

After the passing of the Municipal Reform Act in 1835, Devonport elected its first full town council in 1837, and chose as its first mayor the Lord of the Manor of Stoke Damerel, Edward St Aubyn. The three towns were contiguous, and throughout the expansion of the nineteenth century there was increasing pressure on all available space. Eventual amalgamation was increasingly inevitable, and only a matter of time.

six

Victorian Plymouth

During the nineteenth century there was a rapid increase of population throughout the three towns of Plymouth. This placed great demands on the available housing and utilities, including the water supply, transport services, medical and educational facilities, which the authorities found hard to meet.

A serious shortage of housing exacerbated the overcrowding problem. Between 1841 and 1851 the population of Plymouth increased by over 1,600 a year, partly due to migration from west Devon and Cornwall through agricultural wages being lower than those in the three towns, the agricultural farming depression from 1870 onwards, and the closure of some Cornish mines. According to the 1851 census Plymouth had a population of almost 53,000, Devonport 38,000, and Stonehouse 12,000, and two rear courts, Victory Court and Quarry Court, contained almost 10 per cent of the local Irish population. Victory Court alone housed 133 people, ninety-four of whom were Irish, while in Quarry Court six dwellings were occupied by ninety-five people, eighty of whom were Irish. In the census returns for 1861, of all English ports only Liverpool had a higher Irish population than the three towns. Irish-born residents were concentrated largely in a small district to the north of Millbay, where infant mortality rates were especially high and life expectancy was short. Altogether that year there were over 4,000 Irish people living in Plymouth, Devonport and Stonehouse, of whom about a quarter were servicemen. There was also a strong Irish civilian influx, swelled by those taking advantage of inexpensive journeys by steamer from Dublin to Plymouth.

The building of new houses struggled to contain this rate of increase. In 1850 the average number of people living in each house in Britain was five, but in Plymouth it was ten; in some parts of the town the rate was even higher, with houses at the top of New Street accommodating an average of twenty-four people. Rooms in some houses were subdivided, with one privy often serving a whole block. Water supply sometimes consisted of only one standpipe, operating one hour a day to supply an entire court. The worst slum areas were to be found in Stonehouse, around Long Street, and in the New Street and Breton Side area of Plymouth.

Such a heavily overpopulated area was naturally vulnerable to disease. A severe outbreak of cholera took its toll of the country in 1832, and in Plymouth it claimed 1,031 lives, 211 in one week in August alone. Another epidemic in 1849 killed 1,894, and in 1850 a government inquiry was ordered as the annual mortality in Plymouth for the last seven years had been over twenty-three for every thousand. An outbreak of smallpox in 1872 claimed 448 lives. Such pandemics increased pressure for the municipal authorities to build a proper system of drains and sewers. In 1847, there

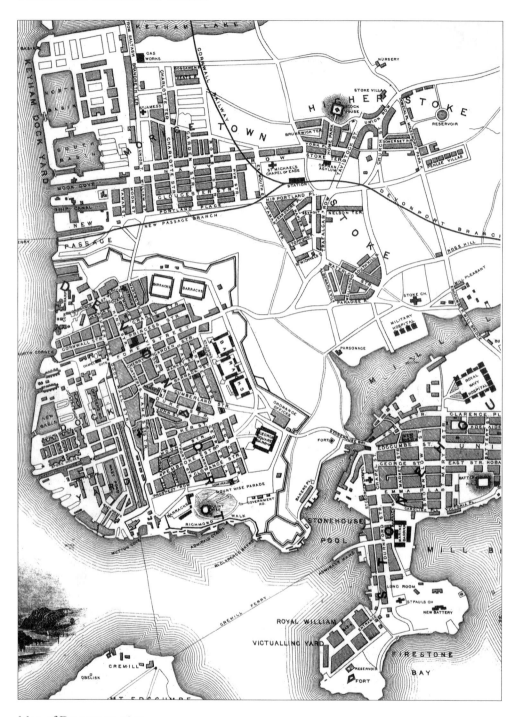

Map of Devonport, 1850.

had been no drains in twenty-seven Plymouth streets, which had a total of 3,300 inhabitants between them. Local government board inspectors claimed that Plymouth and Devonport ranked with Warsaw as the most unsanitary towns in Europe. One observer wrote that almost every room in some of the poorest areas was 'crammed with wretched, beastly and degraded creatures, swarming with vermin and wallowing in filth.' Drunkenness was endemic, and it was estimated that in Morice Town, beside the dockyard, every third building was an inn.

A Unitarian minister, the Revd W. Odgers, was primarily responsible for the opening of public bath houses in Hoegate Street in 1850. Health provision for the community had begun to improve some years earlier with the opening of an eye hospital at Millbay in 1821, becoming the Royal Eye Infirmary in 1828. The South Devon and East Cornwall Hospital at Notte Street opened in 1840 with twelve beds, followed by the Royal Albert Hospital at Devonport in 1862. In 1854 Plymouth adopted the 1848 Public Health Act, which aimed to improve the sanitary condition of towns in England and Wales by giving local corporations full responsibility for the supply of water, sewerage, drainage, cleansing and paving. This led to the installation of better drains, streets being widened and the poorest houses demolished. In turn this exacerbated the ever-present problem of making enough housing available, as slum clearance placed greater pressure on the need for better housing. The matter was addressed by the Housing of the Working Class Act of 1890, which compelled local authorities to act. Plymouth Council set up a Housing Committee, and the first council houses were built in 1896 in Laira Bridge Road. In Devonport a private Dockyard Dwelling Co. was formed to begin a series of slum clearance schemes. Pressure on housing resulted in gaps between and within the towns being infilled, as well as an outward spread into the surrounding countryside.

The site of Stonehouse had always been very cramped, with little space for further development. It was squeezed in between Plymouth and Stonehouse Creek, with buildings such as the Royal Marine Barracks, the Victualling Yard and the Royal Naval Hospital occupying much of the area, and it acquired its local board, which became an urban council in 1894. During the nineteenth century, all available spaces in the Durnford area were infilled with small working class houses, and when the old Sourpool marshes were drained, houses extended eastwards towards Plymouth.

The growth of Plymouth was restricted to an extent by a number of large private estates. The Barley House estate, which extended from King Street to North Road, only became available for development in the late 1860s, while on the east, adjoining Beaumont Park, a family estate belonging to the Culme-Seymour family was not developed until the end of the nineteenth century. Housing therefore had to spread north to North Road and Cobourg Street, up to North Hill and down Alexandra Road and along Mutley Plain. More substantial residences were built from Mannamead down Townsend Hill to Hyde Park Corner, and several surrounding villages were absorbed into Plymouth.

A new Guildhall was built beside St Andrew's Church and completed in 1873. Several churches were built around the middle of the century, among them Holy Trinity in 1840, Christ Church in 1845, St James in 1861 and King Street Methodist Church in 1864. Baptist churches were built at George Street in 1845 and Mutley in 1864, and in the latter year a Congregationalist Church was built at Sherwell. In 1832 the national schools won government grants, and churches in all three towns began to found their own schools in the next twenty years.

The gateway to the Royal William Victualling Yard, surmounted by Sir John Rennie's statue of King William IV.

In 1870 the Education Act required local authorities to establish elected, rate-levying school boards and provide schools for all, though attendance was not compulsory until 1876 and education was not free until 1891. By 1903 Plymouth had built eighteen schools and Devonport nine. A high school for girls had been established in 1874 and one for boys in 1878; the latter amalgamated with the Mannamead School in 1896 to become Plymouth College and remained independent. Devonport High School for Boys was also established in 1896, while Devonport High School for Girls was founded in 1911. Plymouth and Devonport both celebrated the Queen's Golden Jubilee in 1887 by incorporating existing art and science schools into technical colleges, with new buildings completed by Plymouth in 1892 and Devonport in 1899. In 1880 the Royal Naval Engineering College, situated alongside the dockyard wall at Keyham, was opened as 'the training school for engineer students.'

In Devonport Agnes ('Aggie') Weston, a former worker with the Royal Naval Temperance Society, opened the first of her Sailors' Rests close to the dockyard gates at Fore Street, Devonport in 1876. It contained a service restaurant and a hostel, and naturally no alcohol was served on the premises.

In 1834, at a meeting at Plymouth Guildhall, £20,000 was subscribed to build the Plymouth, Devonport & Exeter Railway. Ten years later the Plymouth Co., later the South Devon Railway, was created by Act of Parliament. The first railway of any kind in Plymouth had been the Eddystone tramway, built in 1756 to assist with carrying stone while the lighthouse was under construction. In August 1812 a similar system, the Breakwater tramway, was laid from Oreston Quarry to the pierhead for taking stone to the Plymouth Breakwater. A need to transport granite blocks from quarries on Dartmoor had led to the building of the Plymouth & Dartmoor Railway in 1823, with a branch of that line opened to Cann Quarry in 1829 and a branch to Plympton opened in 1833. The Bristol & Exeter Railway was already under construction in 1836 when Isambard Kingdom Brunel surveyed a line through the South Hams to Plymouth. Lord Morley's consulting engineer, James Meadows Rendel, had previously surveyed a line through the heart of Dartmoor to Plymouth. In October 1840 a meeting was held at the Royal Hotel, at which the proposal made by Rendel was considered, namely that a route across the moor would be several miles shorter than the line through Totnes and cost over £1,000 less to construct. His recommendation was accepted but with little interest, and in 1842 the plan was rejected in favour of a line to the south of the moor based on Brunel's survey. This became known as the Plymouth, Devonport & Exeter Railway until November 1843, when the name was changed to the South Devon Railway.

On 5 May 1848 the South Devon Railway was opened between Totnes and a temporary station at Laira Green, on the outskirts of Plymouth, a route which forms the present main line into Plymouth. It was extended to Millbay Station in April 1849. The South Devon Railway was taken over by the Great Western Railway in 1876. In May 1853 a new branch of the South Devon Railway was opened from a junction at Laira to Sutton Harbour. With the expansion of the railways, coaching services declined accordingly.

The Royal Albert Bridge, sometimes known as the Brunel or Saltash Bridge, was built in 1859, spanning the River Tamar and Saltash on the Cornish bank, and carrying the Cornish main line in and out of Cornwall. It was designed in 1855 by Isambard Kingdom Brunel for the Cornwall Railway Co. – after Parliament had rejected his original plan for a train ferry across the Hamoaze – and was opened by Albert, Prince Consort, on 2 May 1859.

A Plymouth tram. (Courtesy of M. Richards)

Devonport railway station, which was opened in May 1859. Between 1948 and 1968 it was known as Devonport Albert Road railway station to distinguish it from Devonport Kings Road station, which was later demolished and is now the site of City College, Plymouth.

The Prince and Princess of Wales on the royal yacht *Osborne*, November 1865.

During her long life Queen Victoria only paid two visits to Plymouth. The first was in July 1833, when as fourteen-year-old heiress to the throne she and he mother, the Duchess of Kent, stopped at the town on a cruise along the south coast, and Princess Square was later named in her honour. In August 1843 the Queen, Prince Albert and their court took the royal yacht *Victoria & Albert* on its maiden voyage whilst paying a visit to King Louis-Philippe of France. On their way they enjoyed a cruise along the south coast of England, and put in at Plymouth Sound. They received deputations from the Corporations of Plymouth and Devonport on board, and Prince Albert was invested with the office of Lord High Steward. Later that day they visited the dockyard, from where carriages took them for a drive at a foot's pace all over the Three Towns. The streets were so packed, the press reported that 'it would have been possible to walk upon their heads,' and the noise was described as quite deafening.

The Queen's eldest son Albert Edward, Prince of Wales, later Edward VII, was a more frequent visitor. In July 1860 he sailed from Plymouth Sound to Canada and the United States, where he was to undertake a tour lasting four months. In November 1865 he and the Princess of Wales anchored on the royal yacht *Osborne* at Barnpool in torrential rain, visited the Royal Agricultural Show at Pennycomequick, and the Tamar Bridge, and attended a ball in the officers' mess at Royal William Yard. In August 1874 the Prince returned to the town to open the new Guildhall and municipal buildings. The Guildhall's row of stained-glass double windows recorded famous passages in Plymouth's history, the last representing the opening ceremony itself, with the heir to the throne resplendent in frock coat and top hat.

Derry's Clock was, and remains, one of the great Victorian landmarks of the town. Its history goes back to 1862 when William Derry, mayor of Plymouth, presented the town with a clock worth £220 and a half of the cost of the coloured limestone tower in which to display it. The Corporation had no legal authority to construct a clock tower although it was permitted to build a fountain, so the authorities went ahead with a construction comprising three fountains. Although it has never been linked to any water supply it is officially a fountain, yet still known as Derry's Clock. £300 was raised by public subscription to build it, and Derry paid the remainder. It was built with four illuminated dials, each 4ft in diameter, with a 15ft pendulum. The tower is held in such high affection by true Plymothians that suggestions over the years to have it moved to another more prominent position have always met with strong objections. Until the Second World War it stood at a major junction of George Street, Union Street, Lockyer Street and George Place, and was regarded as the centre of Plymouth. All the trams and buses terminated nearby, and there was a local saying that marriages may be made in heaven – but in Plymouth they are arranged under Derry's Clock.

As alternatives to rail transport, there were steamers on the River Tamar from around 1839 onwards. John Gilbert of Saltash owned the Saltash & Three Towns Steamboat Co., which had a mixed fleet of eight or nine paddlers and screw vessels. There were steamers to supplement the Torpoint Ferry from 1895 to 1932, and steamers on the Cremyll Ferry from 1885. There was an Oreston & Turnchapel service on the Cattewater from 1871, moving to Phoenix Wharf when the latter was built in 1895.

In 1832 horse-drawn buses began running in Plymouth. One of the first horse tramways in Britain, which began in March 1872, linked Devonport with Plymouth. The first route was from Derry's Clock, through Stonehouse to Cumberland Gardens, Devonport, with passing places at Devonport Hill, Stonehouse Bridge and in Union Street, run on a 4ft 8½in gauge single track line by the Plymouth, Stonehouse and Devonport Tramways Co. This line was extended to the centre of Devonport in 1874 by a one-way system inwards up Chapel Street and outwards via St Aubyn Street. In 1880 the Plymouth, Devonport & District Tramways Co. was set up, initially operating five steam locomotives hauling open-top cars, running a single line from Millbay Station via George Street, Lockyer Street, Princess Square, Bedford Street, Cobourg Street and Houndiscombe Road, terminating at Hyde Park Corner. Nearby residents complained about the smells, noise and smoke which ensued, and its poor timekeeping soon lost it much of its initial clientele. A year later it was sold to the Plymouth Tramways Co., and in 1892 it changed hands again, becoming the Plymouth Corporation Tramway Department. It extended its routes in 1893 from Millbay Station to the Hoe and pier and from Mutley Plain to Compton Lane End.

Local train services were started by the London & South Western Railway from St Budeaux to the Dockyard in 1890 and from Plymouth to Turnchapel and Yealmpton in 1897, and the Great Western Railway introduced a series of stops on its journeys between Saltash and Plympton in 1904. Ferries often linked with the railway network, one such link being the service operated by the steamer *Kitley Belle* from the Steer Point Halt down the Yealm Estuary to Newton Ferrers and Noss Mayo.

The Plymouth Stonehouse & Devonport Tramways Co. Ltd was the first to be established under the 1870 Act, which aimed to promote this new means of transport by clarifying and regulating the legal position for local authorities. Tramlines were laid from Derry's Clock along Union Street to Cumberland Road by 1872, and were extended to Fore Street two years later. Within ten years Plymouth trams were carrying a million passengers every year. The early trams were horse-drawn, but in 1884 the Tramways Co. ran steam trams for two years on a route through the town from Millbay to Hyde Park Corner. Within five years the steam engines were replaced by horses.

Trams in Fore Street, Devonport, 1909.

Mutley Plain, *c.* 1905.

The Corporation bought the company out in 1892, and within a year Plymouth Corporation Tramways had extended the line at each end to the Promenade Pier and Compton Lane End at the junction of Tavistock Road and Eggbuckland Road, popularly known at the time as Hender's Corner (a name derived from the large seed and flower nurseries nearby). In 1896 it opened a second route, to Prince Rock, as the Corporation was building a power station there which would electrify the tramway system, give Plymouth its first street lights, and eventually the whole power system.

In September 1899 the mayor, Alderman John Pethick, opened the Plymouth Corporation Electricity Works and inaugurated the first of the electric trams. Plymouth now had its own public electricity system a few years after several other towns of similar size, though Devonport and Stonehouse had to wait another two years before being connected to the grid. The streets had been lit by gas since 1832 and the first demonstration of electric light was provided in 1849, when an arc lamp was installed at the top of the Devonport Column. However, the first significant local use of electric light was for the illumination of the Promenade Pier, which was opened in May 1884.

As the outer districts of Plymouth rapidly expanded, a double-track extension was built in 1905 to Peverell Park Road. The Devonport & District Tramway became a subsidiary of the British Electric Traction Group and started an electric network in 1901, running from Devonport to the developing areas of Millbridge, Stoke, Keyham and Camels Head. Power came from the Devonport Corporation power station in Newport Street, Stonehouse, through the multi-station built to blend with the architecture of Devonport Technical School.

At around the end of the century the motor bus appeared. The Plymouth Motor Co. started a service in 1900 between Derry's Clock and Salisbury Road with five Daimlers. In 1909 Peverell Road Car Co. ran buses on the Milehouse and Stoke route, garaging them in Outland Mills at the junction of Lyndhurst and Milehouse Roads, but ceased operations in 1911 due to lack of business. Until the First World War in 1914, Plymouth street transport was dominated by the electric tram. Free movement was obstructed by the toll gates, left over from the days of turnpikes, and by the mid-nineteenth century the cost of collecting tolls was greater than the amount yielded. The gates at Milehouse, Mutley Plain and Cattedown Corner were removed in the 1850s. Plymouth Corporation purchased the Iron Bridge and the Embankment in 1897, retaining the toll gates in order to help recoup the cost. The tolls at Mill Bridge and Stonehouse Bridge had been sold by the Edgcumbes to the General Tolls Co. in 1890, although the Earl of Mount Edgcumbe and Lord St Levan retained shares in the latter. Plymouth Town Council purchased the toll rights for £100,000 in 1923, a measure which would have allowed the town to charge tolls for the next ten years. Nevertheless a decision was made to abolish them altogether, probably because the expense of collecting them exceeded the revenue raised. This was done on 1 April 1924 when the mayor, Solomon Stephens, made a ceremonial tour of the four remaining toll houses to declare that they would now be toll-free.

The road running east to Plymstock was improved with the construction of an iron bridge over the Laira Estuary. It was designed by James Rendel and opened in 1827, and was at the time the second longest iron bridge in the country. As it was impossible to bridge some of the creeks and inlets, so new ferry services were built at Phoenix Wharf, Hooe, Oreston and Turnchapel. In 1877 a new railway station was opened at North Road.

The first public library was opened in Plymouth on 30 August 1876 in the old Guildhall building in Whimple Street, after the new Guildhall was opened.

Stonehouse Bridge, *c.* 1910.

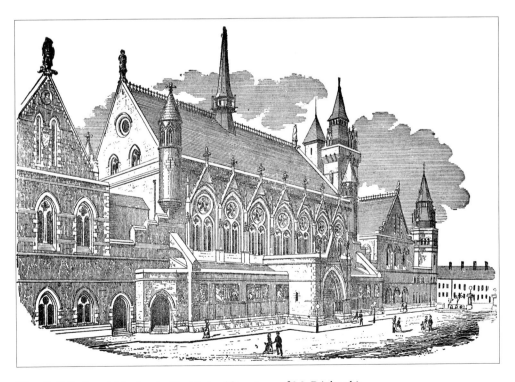

The Guildhall and Mechanics' Institute. (Courtesy of M. Richards)

Plymouth Central Library, Art Gallery and Museum, *c.* 1910, looking up towards North Hill.

William Wright, who had previously maintained libraries for the Plymouth Working Mens' Association and the South Devon Railway Servants, was appointed librarian and the collection initially had a book stock of about 900 volumes. Loans began at the end of September, and between then and July 1878, 186,000 volumes were lent, at a rate of about 400 per day. It also provided a reading room, stocked with newspapers and periodicals. By 1899 it contained about 25,000 volumes in the lending library and about 20,000 in the reference library on the upper floor, as well as special collections of published works, prints and sketches relating to Devon and Cornwall, and patent specifications. Larger premises were needed and Wright persuaded the benefactor, Andrew Carnegie, to contribute £15,000 to the erection of a new central library in Tavistock Road. Work was started on the site in 1907, and the new Central Library, as well as the new City Museum and Art Gallery, were opened in a dual ceremony by the mayor, Alderman J. Yeo, in October 1910. The latter was a successor to the first Plymouth museum, part of the Plymouth Institution, which had been opened in the Athenaeum building, next to the Theatre Royal, and completed in 1829.

By the end of the twentieth century, the City Museum and Art Gallery was home to major collections of fine and decorative arts, natural and human history. Over 150,000 specimens of insects, birds, mammals, skeletons, plants, fossils and rocks comprised the natural history collection, in addition to a large natural history library and archive. There were also many important prehistoric artefacts from Dartmoor, Bronze and Iron-Age material from Mount Batten, medieval and post-medieval discoveries from Plymouth, as well as artefacts from Ancient Egypt and other ancient cultures of Europe and the Middle East. The fine arts included works from the sixteenth to the twentieth centuries, numbering around 750 easel paintings, over 3,000 watercolours and drawings, over 5,000 prints, sculptures, and work by local artists including Sir Joshua Reynolds, the Victorian landscape painter Frederick Richard Lee, and artists of the Newlyn School, the St Ives group of painters and works by the Camden Town Group.

Limited space only allowed for a small amount of the permanent collection to be seen at any one time, a problem alleviated to some extent by regular rotating displays.

The Marine Biological Association was formed in 1884, and Plymouth was chosen as the site for its laboratory and aquarium because of its diversity of flora and fauna. A site under the Royal Citadel was offered by the War Department in order to maintain direct salt-water contact. The aquarium opened the following year, and soon built up an international reputation for scientific research.

Since the early eighteenth century several local newspapers had been started, though they generally had a short life. In the early nineteenth century the *Plymouth and Dock Weekly Journal*, which was founded in 1819 and changed its name five years later to the *Plymouth and Devonport Weekly Journal*, was the most popular. On 3 January 1860, five years after abolition of the tax on newspapers, the town's first daily, the *Western Morning News*, made its first appearance. Published from offices in George Street, it strove to maintain a politically independent stance, although with broadly Liberal sympathies. 'In matters of Politics and Religion we shall be strictly independent,' the editorial of the first issue promised. 'We do not hold a brief for any party, in Church or State.' Six months later the rival *Western Daily Mercury*, based in Frankfort Gate, a more unashamedly Liberal journal, published its first issue. It took over the *Weekly Journal*, and in 1895 launched another daily, the *Western Evening Herald*. Always ready to rise to a challenge from rivals, the *Western Morning News* promptly launched its own *Western Evening News* which, however, only lasted a few months. Tragically the founding editor of the *Western Morning News*, Edward Spender, and his two small sons were drowned in a bathing accident while on holiday in Whitsand Bay in June 1878.

Two of Plymouth's leading journalists of the era were to make their mark as ranking among the town's major historians. Richard Norsworthy Worth joined the *Western Morning News* staff in 1860 as a reporter, leaving five years later to become a newspaper editor in Newcastle but returning to his home town not long afterwards. In 1872 he published the first edition of his *History of Plymouth*, with a second corrected edition following two years later and a considerably enlarged one appearing in 1890. His interests also embraced geology and archaeology, both of which were included in the latter edition, and in his later years he worked for the Plymouth book printers Messrs Brendon & Sons, with whom he remained until his death in 1897.

In 1900 Henry Francis Whitfeld, editor at various times of the *Western Daily Mercury* and *Western Independent*, published *Plymouth and Devonport in Times of War and Peace*. A committed Liberal, Whitfeld had campaigned against slum conditions in Plymouth, and while editing the *Independent*, wrote a series of articles on the parlous state of housing in Devonport. They led indirectly to the formation of the Private Dockyard Dwelling Co., and he was elected chairman of Devonport Corporation's Housing Committee, which launched a slum clearance programme.

The third great local historian of the Victorian era, Llewellynn Jewitt, was also Librarian of Plymouth Proprietary Library, financed by members' subscriptions, and his *History of Plymouth* was published in 1872. He was angry when Worth's volume was issued while his own was still in preparation. Suspecting dirty tricks, Jewitt wrote scathingly in his introduction of 'the total disregard of literary etiquette by its compiler who, while a work long announced was passing through the press … actually attempted to forestall it by one of his own,' concluding that it was 'not worth my while to remark.'

During the Victorian era, Plymouth Hoe was almost doubled in extent and laid out with gardens and paths. In the process it became one of the finest promenades in the

Devonport Park, *c.* 1910.

country, and one early twentieth-century writer, S.P.B. Mais, could write that England 'has no more majestic sight than that which catches the eye as one emerges on her vast Hoe.' It became a site for monuments and war memorials, with Sir Edgar Boehm's statue of Drake, a replica of one at Tavistock, erected in 1884 and the foundation stone of the Armada memorial laid on the tercentenary date, 21 July 1888. The latter was unveiled on 21 October 1890 by Alfred, Duke of Edinburgh, the second son of Queen Victoria and Commander-in-Chief at Devonport from 1890 to 1893. The Duke of Edinburgh had long been an enthusiastic amateur violinist. During his three years in office he joined the Orchestral Society conducted by Dr Samuel Weekes, and was one of the violinists who regularly played in concerts at the Guildhall. He also obtained for Plymouth a visit and two concerts from the Royal Orchestral Society, of which he was president.

Several other public parks and recreation grounds were to be found elsewhere in the Three Towns. Devonport Park was created and first opened about 1858, redeveloped and underwent improvements in layout some thirty years later and was officially reopened in 1895. During the very hot summer in 1887 the mill pool for Stonehouse Mills, otherwise known as the Deadlake, became a serious health hazard for local residents, who organised a petition which was presented to the three local authorities of Plymouth, Devonport and Stonehouse. The latter agreed to a joint purchase of the Deadlake from the Earl of Mount Edgcumbe in 1890 and to filling it in, and it was first opened as a park in 1891. It was still far from complete; in 1895 several hundred tons of rubble from the old tram depot at Compton were poured into it, and tipping continued over the next ten years. Soon after it was renamed Victoria Park in 1898, residents were complaining to the authorities about children playing football and other games there on Sundays. Four years later it was complete, and the mayor, Joseph Bellamy, performed the official opening ceremony in October 1902.

Nearer the centre of Plymouth was Beaumont Park, comprising the grounds of Beaumont House, near Tothill, and St Jude's Church. In 1882 the Revd Thomas Bewes, who had lived in the house for over twenty years, purchased a strip of private land alongside in order to extend his garden. He stipulated in the deeds to his house that it was to be held until acquired by Plymouth with the rest of the park. After his death in 1890, the trustees sold the house and park to the Corporation for £26,000, and it was opened to the public in May 1892. Another recreational area was to be found at the smaller Westwell Gardens, formerly the burial ground for St Andrew's Church. It was opened in 1901 but destroyed during the Blitz forty years later, and the site now lies under the new Guildhall. Regular social activities for all included annual races in August at Chelson Meadow, and a fair around the market in November.

A growing network of reservoirs was created for the town, with Sherwell established in the 1820s, and additional ones at Crownhill in 1851, Hartley in 1860, and Roborough in 1885. Daily consumption in 1893 was estimated at 4.5 million gallons and Plymouth needed still more water, particularly as it was vulnerable during extremely cold weather with the possibility of the open leat from Dartmoor freezing, as it had done in 1881. Another reservoir to serve the three towns but nearer the moor was required, and Burrator was opened in 1898.

A Committee of Harbour Defences, set up in 1844, recommended that at Plymouth three new batteries should be constructed on the coast at Plymouth. In 1852 the French President, Louis Napoleon, proclaimed himself Emperor Napoleon III. During the Crimean War England and France had been united in friendship, but when relations between both countries deteriorated a few years later old fears about a possible French invasion resurfaced, and forts were built on the landward side of the town, and a Militia Act was passed to establish a territorial army. When the French enlarged their dockyard at Cherbourg on the northern coast, and when Napoleon III declared war on Austria in 1859 and launched the world's first armour-plated steam-driven warship, the government suspected that Britain could be threatened by future military action. That same year it passed a Volunteer Act, which included the creation of twenty-four Rifle Corps in the County of Devon and some twelve Artillery Corps, and set up a Royal Commission to examine the state of national defences.

In 1860 work was begun on improving defence structures at Picklecombe, Bovisand and Drake's Island. Expenditure on these and similar projects soon exceeded the budget, and the contractor who had been employed to construct the defences around Plymouth's north-eastern boundary went bankrupt. A fort was being constructed just off the Breakwater, and in 1866 a decision was made to complete it in iron rather than masonry. Several more batteries were built during the next few years. However in 1870 France was defeated by Germany in the Franco-Prussian War, the French empire fell, and after his abdication the exiled Napoleon III came to settle in Kent for the last two years of his life. In 1871 he spent a holiday at Torquay and came briefly to Plymouth. A curious crowd on Plymouth Hoe surrounded his carriage and he had to forego his intended promenade. As for the new defence works, now largely redundant, they acquired the name of 'Palmerston's Follies'.

In the nineteenth century the dockyard still dominated industry in Plymouth. Paddle steamers had always been vulnerable to attack in times of war and were gradually being replaced by the first ironclad ships with screw propellers. As the change in ship types required a change in dock facility, the dockyard was extended from 1844 onwards when work was started on the Keyham steam yard for building steam ships and completed ten years later. The Great Western Docks designed by Isambard Kingdom Brunel were built between 1844 and 1850. Plymouth's commercial importance was underlined by the fact

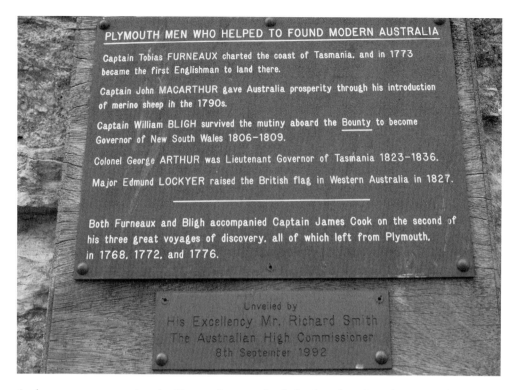

PLYMOUTH MEN WHO HELPED TO FOUND MODERN AUSTRALIA

Captain Tobias FURNEAUX charted the coast of Tasmania, and in 1773 became the first Englishman to land there.

Captain John MACARTHUR gave Australia prosperity through his introduction of merino sheep in the 1790s.

Captain William BLIGH survived the mutiny aboard the Bounty to become Governor of New South Wales 1806–1809.

Colonel George ARTHUR was Lieutenant Governor of Tasmania 1823–1836.

Major Edmund LOCKYER raised the British flag in Western Australia in 1827.

Both Furneaux and Bligh accompanied Captain James Cook on the second of his three great voyages of discovery, all of which left from Plymouth, in 1768, 1772, and 1776.

Unveiled by
His Excellency Mr. Richard Smith
The Australian High Commissioner
8th September 1992

A plaque commemorating the Plymouth men who helped to found modern Australia. (© Kim Van der Kiste)

that in the second half of the nineteenth century liners travelling to North America, South Africa, Australia and New Zealand began calling in at the port, and it also became one of the foremost departure points in England for emigrants. In 1853 the inner defences of Devonport, halted in 1816, were completed, and the old squares behind the lines were replaced by Raglan Barracks, built between 1854 and 1858, and named after the commander in the Crimean War. During the latter conflict, Devonport was kept busy building and repairing warships, and despatching troops to the front.

The South Devon Militia had new barracks built on the edge of Plymouth, at Mutley, in 1840. With the Napoleonic scare the local volunteer regiment, which had been disbanded in 1814, was reformed and the Plymouth battalion was the second most senior in the country. Their headquarters were demolished to make way for the new Guildhall, and a new drill hall was built in 1870 on the southern side of the old Millbay prisoner-of-war barracks. The Durnford Street block of the Royal Marines Barracks was added in 1867, doubling the size of the establishment. In the late 1850s the docks in South Yard were reshaped and enlarged to cope with the new steam vessels. Naval needs were changing, as ships were changing from floating gun platforms into complex vessels with new weapons and armour, innovations which led to the building of the Royal Naval Engineering College. The fleet was outgrowing the existing yards, and in 1896 an extension at Keyham was started, adding another 130 acres to the existing 140 acres of dockyard. Another small township, East Stonehouse, had been growing between Plymouth and the Dock, and became the site of several military establishments as well as the development of the commercial docks at Millbay.

Royal Naval Barracks, Devonport, *c.* 1840.

Royal Naval Barracks, Devonport, *c.* 1900.

The Duke of Cornwall Hotel. (© Kim Van der Kiste)

The Barbican, *c.* 1865.

In 1844, brothers William and James Bryant went into partnership with John Burnell and established a soap factory in Sutton Road. William Bryant and Edward James had already built a sugar refinery in Mill Lane in 1838, and this was sold in 1856 to the British & Irish Sugar Refining Co. Edward James began a starch factory in Sutton Road, and established a close personal friendship with Isaac Reckitt of Hull, whose firm took over the Plymouth factory in 1905. The Bryant-Burnell soap works had become the West of England Soap Works in 1857, and this was taken over in 1863 by the Victoria Soap Co., started in 1858 at Millbay. All production was concentrated there until 1896, when competition from the nearby Millbay Co. resulted in the Victoria Soap Co. going out of business and being taken over by the New Patent Candle Co.

Mill Lane, Morice Town, Millbay and Coxside were by now established as the main industrial areas of Plymouth. The industrialist Thomas Gill quarried limestone at Millbay, taking his workings right up to the edge of the corporation land on the Hoe. By 1880 the terraces of houses had been built on the quarry floor, and West Hoe Park was later established under the quarry cliff face. With the growth of liner and rail traffic during the middle of the century, there was a pressing need for hotel accommodation. Three were built in the Millbay area, the Duke of Cornwall in 1863, the Albion Hotel in 1875, which became the Albion and Continental when it took over the Royal Eye Infirmary premises in 1904, and the Grand Hotel on the Hoe in 1880.

Other industries included brewing, civilian shipbuilding, soap making, glass making, printing and fishing. The printing firm of Latimer and Brendon opened in the mid-nineteenth century, and a new fish market on the Barbican was built in 1896. The Scott brothers, one of whom was a grandfather of the Antarctic explorer Robert Falcon Scott, purchased the Hoegate brewery in 1826. Three main breweries in the Devonport area merged into the Tamar Brewery at Morice Town, and a group of Plymouth brewers was merged into Plymouth Breweries in 1889, concentrating in the former Regent Brewery, Stonehouse. Both were later taken over by the Courage empire.

One of the town's most interesting trading stories was that of Stanley Gibbons, who was apprenticed while still an adolescent to his father's business as a chemist in the family shop at Treville Street. In 1856 he took advantage of rapidly growing interest in the new hobby of philately, or stamp collecting, when he started selling postage stamps from a desk in the corner of the shop. Seven years later he purchased two large sacks of Cape of Good Hope triangular stamps for £5 from two visiting sailors who had just won them in a raffle, and subsequently made a profit of about £500 on selling them to customers. In 1865 he published his first price list, which was in effect the first Gibbons stamp catalogue, and on his father's death in 1867 he took over the pharmaceutical business. In the 1871 census he was described as a 'chemist and dealer in foreign stamps'. He sold the pharmaceutical concern the following year and moved to larger premises in Lockyer Street. Although he moved to London in 1874, it is interesting to consider that the world's major trader in what was for years a most popular hobby had its roots in a shop in Plymouth.

Ever since the Great Reform Act of 1832 Plymouth and Devonport had both returned two Members of Parliament. Plymouth had long had a non-conformist tradition that could be traced back to its siding with the Puritans and Oliver Cromwell during the Civil War. However, Conservatism tended to hold sway because of its identification with patriotism and identification with the armed forces, particularly during the nineteenth century, and the people of Plymouth generally elected one, if not two Conservatives. One exception to the rule was Robert Collier, a merchant of Quaker extraction from the long-established local corn and timber merchants Collier & Co. of Southside Street. He became Liberal Member in 1852, and later held office as Solicitor-General and Attorney-General. The Devonport Members were normally Liberals, except during 1874 to 1892 when the Conservatives held both seats, a feat they repeated in 1910.

Off the coast it was realised that if Smeaton's Tower was left standing in its existing location, it would be a constant danger to the new lighthouse, because if the rock was to give way there was a severe risk of it crashing into the new lighthouse. When Trinity House Board threatened to blow it up, a suggestion was made that Smeaton's Tower should instead be dismantled stone by stone and re-erected on Plymouth Hoe to replace the Trinity House navigation obelisk. In 1877 Sir James Douglass, Engineer-in-Chief to Trinity House, announced a decision to rebuild the lighthouse on a more solid foundation to the south-east. At a public meeting, £1,200 was raised by subscription, and it was completed in 1882.

In 1879 a body of Royal Marines from Stonehouse and other units was sent out to Africa during the Boer War, and crowds cheered on the seafront as the ship *Jumna* sailed out to sea. Major Chard of St Budeaux subsequently led the defence of Rorke's Drift; he was awarded the Victoria Cross. Twenty years later, many young men from Plymouth were fighting in the ranks of the 2nd Devon Volunteer Battalion in the Second Boer War in South Africa.

A memorial to soldiers who had died in the conflict was unveiled in 1903 near the entrance to the Royal Citadel. It was presented to Plymouth by Alfred Mosely of London, a merchant in South Africa who had chosen the town as a fitting location for a memorial because of his family ties with Devon. He dedicated it to Prince Christian

Smeaton's Tower and bandstand on Plymouth Hoe. (Courtesy of M. Richards)

The Boer War Memorial.
(© Kim Van der Kiste)

Victor, a grandson of Queen Victoria, who had served with distinction but died of fever in South Africa in 1900, and to the officers and men of the Devonshire, Somerset and Gloucestershire Regiments who were killed in the fighting. Mosely had been responsible for setting up the field hospital at Natal during the campaign where Prince Christian Victor had died. The memorial, 43ft high, comprises a shaft of red granite mounted on a green base and with steps and pillars of grey Devonshire granite, with bronze panels on the sides and base.

In the mid-nineteenth century the new suburb of Morice Town was built outside Devonport. At the end of the century further expansion took place when Compton Gifford was absorbed by Plymouth in 1896 and part of the village of St Budeaux the following year. In 1898 another part of St Budeaux was added to Devonport, and part of Pennycross was absorbed by St Budeaux. Part of Weston Peverell was added to Devonport in 1900. Saltash Passage, previously in Cornwall, became part of Plymouth, which by the early twentieth century extended from Tothill to Lipson, Prince Rock to Cattedown, Mutley to Mannamead and to Peverell Park Road.

The twentieth century would see an acceleration in the pace of change, much of this dictated by world events. For the greater part of its history, the development of Plymouth had been shaped by its role in the defence of the nation from the Hundred Years' War and the Spanish Armada to the foundation of the dockyard and the campaign against France in the age of Napoleon. The devastation of total war would soon see the city, as it had become by then, completely transformed within a very short space of time.

seven

Plymouth 1901–39

In 1901 Plymouth had a population of 107,000, while Devonport had almost 64,000 and Stonehouse 15,000. With the end of the Victorian era and the advent on what in retrospect was seen as the Edwardian age – generally reckoned as the thirteen years which ended with the outbreak of the First World War in August 1914 – there were unsettling portents of the shape of things to come throughout Britain, and the effects were felt in Plymouth as much as anywhere else in the country.

With the naval arms race, in which Germany sought to try and build a superior fleet to its rival across the North Sea, Devonport dockyard had its role in national affairs. In March 1902 King Edward VII and Queen Alexandra paid a visit to Devon to lay the foundation stone for the Dartmouth Royal Naval College, and then to the dockyard at Devonport to launch the battleship HMS *Queen*, and to lay the keel-plate of *King Edward VII*, to be launched in 1903.

Plymouth and Devonport thus had an important part in the Anglo-German naval arms race which dominated the minds of sovereigns, politicians and governments on both sides of the North Sea. The German Emperor William II, 'Kaiser Bill', King Edward's nephew, had also visited the town in his early days, probably in 1871 when he was a boy of twelve. In his memoirs, he wrote years later that while staying on the Isle of Wight he visited Portsmouth, and 'that much more important and extensive port, Plymouth,' where he 'descended in a diving-bell.'

Like the Emperor, the German naval minister Admiral Alfred von Tirpitz was obsessed with the need to increase German sea power, but at the same time was a somewhat envious admirer of Britain and the Royal Navy. Tirpitz had sometimes visited Plymouth as a young cadet when the Prussian navy used the port as a supply base. In the summer of 1904, shortly after spending a few days in Germany, King Edward invited the German battle fleet to pay a three-day visit to Plymouth. On Sunday 10 July, a gloriously fine day, crowds thronged the Hoe and seafront to see the arrival of the German warships in Plymouth Sound. As the flagship approached its mooring it fired a twenty-one-gun salute, while the Royal Citadel Battery replied 'gun for gun'. As the guns boomed, four German cruisers arrived, followed by an armoured cruiser. They anchored in Plymouth Sound while four cruisers anchored on the Staddon side of the Sound.

Never before had such a powerful foreign naval force visited a British port, and it was regarded as a matter of some concern by some editors of the national press. After the fleet had returned from Plymouth, questions were asked in Parliament of the Civil Lord of the Admiralty whether he was aware that German naval officers had

King Edward VII and Queen Alexandra at Devonport Dockyard, March 1902.

photographed the fortifications and dockyard at Devonport, and if so, what action he proposed to take.

In 1907 the Plymouth Civic Guild of Help was founded after a public meeting in the Guildhall. At the time there were no statutory welfare services, and care of the sick and infirm was the responsibility of the Guardians of the Poor. In its formative years the organisation, later the Plymouth Guild of Social Service, was made up of local volunteers who were keen to help forming district committees to receive requests for financial or practical help, or identify those who needed assistance and ensure it was provided. One case it dealt with in the first year was the family of a man who had emigrated to the colonies, leaving a wife and four children, and the only money coming into the house was 2s earned weekly by the eldest girl. The wife was expecting to go into the workhouse, but the Guild found work for her so she could keep the family together in reasonable comfort. Another was that of a young man who could not afford to buy a pair of glasses which he needed to undertake work offered him, and was loaned money to get his clothes out of pawn so he could accept the job.

In April 1912 the sinking of the RMS *Titanic* on her maiden voyage with the loss of 1,517 lives was met with horror on an international scale. The liner *Carpathia* was sent to the scene of the disaster and rescued over 800 survivors, including a number of West Country passengers. On 28 April the liner *Lapland* arrived in Plymouth Sound with 167 surviving passengers and anchored in Cawsand Bay. The first group, including several women stewardesses, was transferred to the Great Western Railway tender *Sir Richard Grenville*. Instead of sailing directly to Millbay Docks, the *Grenville* cruised

The Scott Memorial, Mount Wise.

around the Sound until the other two tenders with the rest of the surviving passengers had left Lapland. There was a delay in not landing them immediately so as to enable the Board of Trade to serve each person with a subpoena requiring them to give evidence before the Receiver of Wrecks at Plymouth. Millbay Docks was closed and guarded by police, not to bar newspaper reporters from entering, but to prevent the *Titanic* survivors from getting out. When the Seamen's Union learned what was happening, representatives sailed out in a boat alongside the *Grenville* to explain the situation to them, and they said they would refuse to give evidence unless the threat of their illegal detention was removed. Their demands were conceded and they landed at Plymouth where they gave their evidence.

In February 1913 another national tragedy had particular local resonance. Robert Falcon Scott, born at Milehouse, Plymouth, had led an expedition to the Antarctic in January 1912, intent on being the first to reach the South Pole, but he and his men were beaten by the Norwegian explorer Roald Amundsen and his party by just one month. Scott and his team perished on the sub-continent in March, and news of their fate did not reach England until eleven months later. A posthumous knighthood was conferred on Scott, and a memorial to him was erected at Mount Wise in 1928.

The 'votes for women' campaign also affected Plymouth, though only in a minor fashion. In April 1913 the base of Smeaton's Tower was daubed with the slogan 'No security till you give women the vote.' Suffragettes were making a protest prior to a Plymouth visit by Winston Churchill, then First Lord of the Admiralty.

Throughout the nineteenth century, the steady expansion of Plymouth, Devonport and Stonehouse had made amalgamation not only inevitable, but, for many concerned, desirable. The Plymouth Social Democratic Federation and the Three Towns Housing Federation both advocated such a move. There were calls for all three to unite as one from 1888 onwards, and a conference on the subject took place at Stonehouse in 1902, but broke up without reaching any binding resolutions. A meeting of the Plymouth Town Council on 24 November 1913 pressed strongly for negotiations to be opened for amalgamation. A resolution in favour of a memorial to the Local Government Board and negotiation with the Town Council of Devonport, the Devon County Council and the Stonehouse District Committee was moved by the mayor, Thomas Baker, and seconded by his predecessor, James Godding, and was carried by thirty-eight votes to four. A rather different expression of opinion was revealed when Devonport ratepayers were polled and the result was announced on 9 December, recording a vote of 5,032 against amalgamation, with only 2,242 in favour, out of an electorate of over 10,000.

Nevertheless the official bodies were determined to have their way. On 28 January 1914 an enquiry was opened at Plymouth Guildhall by Major C.E. Norton, Local Government Board Inspector, requesting an application for a provisional order for the amalgamation of the county boroughs of Plymouth and Devonport, and the Urban District of East Stonehouse. The application was made by Plymouth Corporation, but opposed by Devonport, while Stonehouse, it was said, was 'adopting a watching attitude.' Representing Plymouth Corporation, Honoratus Lloyd stated that there were three local authorities, but only one town. There was no physical boundary between them, and in all respects but their government they were as one. The result of existing divisions was that difficulties often arose 'through little jealousies and prejudices which prevented the public as a whole being served as it might be.' For example the tramways were worked by Plymouth Corporation, and two independent companies; for the water supply, two authorities drew water from one watershed, each having its own reservoir and pipes, so in practice one authority had water to spare, when the other often had none; and they had three Poor Law authorities and three workhouses; three separate districts for the purpose of maintenance of law and order and the application of justice. In summing up, he thought it was 'little short of an outrage that the Three Towns should continue as they were.'

J.H. Ellis, the town clerk, and Major-General A.P. Penton, Commander of the South Western Coast Defences, both supported the application. The latter had been given permission by the War Office to speak from a military point of view. In peacetime, the general view was that organisation of the three towns into three district bodies was of little importance. During wartime it would be a different matter. In the event of an order for mobilisation, the fortress commander would have to deal with three different authorities instead of one, which would clearly be a waste of time and effort. In view of the ever-increasing German threat to European stability and the possibility that Britain might soon be at war, such a measure could not be postponed much longer. Despite objections from Devonport representatives, the overwhelming mood was in favour of amalgamation.

A provisional order was issued by the Local Government Board for doing so on 2 May 1914, and the Bill confirming the order was passed by a Select Committee of the House of Commons on 15 July, to come into effect in November. The new united borough covered an area of 6,100 acres, with a population of 212,000 and a rateable value of £1.025 million. Such legislation came just at the right time, for within less than a month the government would have far more pressing concerns. On 4 August 1914 Britain declared war on Germany.

Throughout the First World War the dockyard was kept busy; in 1914 it employed over 10,000 men, and by the time peace had been declared the number had grown to almost 19,000. The men's wages were in effect doubled by war bonuses, and supplemented by generous amounts of overtime. Because of the shortage of manpower, large numbers of women were employed in the yard for the first time. Routine repair and maintenance work, repairing damaged ships and fitting out Q-ships in campaigns against the U-boats, meant there was never any shortage of work. There was also a constant need to build new ships. The most famous was the 27,500-ton battleship *Royal Oak*, launched in November 1914 and commissioned on 1 May 1916 to form one of the 4th Battle Squadron at the Battle of Jutland. The ship survived the First World War and lasted until the opening skirmishes of the Second. It also built the cruiser *Cleopatra*, and two K-class submarines, which were designed to steam at the same speed as the battle fleet. On trials in the basin at Keyham, K-6 submerged, but then could not be brought up from the bottom for two hours. Although the faults were repaired by an inspector of engine fitters aboard, the yard men refused to dive in her again.

Prince Rock and other schools were turned into temporary barracks, while Salisbury Road and Hyde Park Road Schools became temporary hospitals. Crowds gathered in September 1914 to see Red Cross trains arriving at Plymouth bringing British and German casualties. Many children suddenly found they had unexpectedly longer holidays. The education authorities were frustrated by a shortage of caretakers and teachers, many of whom had joined the Services. The commanding officer of Plymouth Fortress ordered that the town's vehicle owners must offer their transport at once to the Army Service Corps, or else their vehicles would be taken from them. Many owners questioned the order, unaware of the military power of compulsory purchase. The commandeered transport was used by Plymouth troops and the western home defences.

Royal Marine detachments from Plymouth were active in various theatres of war, including the Battles of the Falkland Islands and Jutland, and a Plymouth battalion formed part of a Royal Marines brigade serving in Belgium and France. Plymouth was not directly threatened by enemy action, though there were fears that the naval port could come under aerial attack from an enemy force operating from bases in north-west Europe. Reports of Zeppelins approaching south-west England were received, and during the winter of 1916 there was a genuine fear of German airships carrying out raids on Plymouth, as they had done on London and the east coast over a year earlier. In the end Plymouth was never attacked, though there was one false alarm that brought the town to a halt. A naval plane which had not been notified to the military passed up the coast, and an order was sent out to take all defensive measures. During the evening rush hour, all traffic on the town roads and all trains then running came to a complete stop, with crowds trapped in the streets and stations, unable to move for a couple of hours until the mistake was discovered.

Every family in Plymouth was affected directly or indirectly by the mounting casualty lists. All the major sea battles involved Devonport ships and men to some extent, and soldiers from the 2nd Devon Regiment were fighting on the front line in France. While the threat of invasion was slight, the War Office still considered it important to put into operation a precautionary defence scheme. It was, however, thought that the sea approaches to Plymouth were more or less impregnable: the eastern approach was closed by a boom and nets, and the western entrance was heavily guarded. At first a guard was placed on railway bridges and viaducts, and road blocks were set up on all main roads leading to Plymouth, as precautions against spies and saboteurs. However, the town suffered little inconvenience, the sea approaches were never disturbed, and ships passed in and out of the Sound unhindered.

Strict wartime regulations were observed by civilians, and those who did not were subject to penalties. In January 1916 a woman was fined by magistrates for contravening an order under the Defence of the Realm Act by driving a car with headlights in Tavistock Road within six miles of the coast. People were also liable to prosecution under the same order if caught sketching within a similar distance of the sea.

Places of entertainment were little affected by the conflict. In particular the Palace Theatre in Union Street, built in 1898 with a capacity of nearly 2,000, played to full houses, with Marie Lloyd, Lillie Langtry, Adelaide Hall, Rob Wilton and other music hall stars regularly appearing on the stage. As there was a shortage of male actors during the war, some shows were produced as revues with a predominantly female cast.

The arrival of the Canadian Expeditionary Force on 14 October 1914 caused great interest in the town. Comprising a convoy consisting of thirty-three liners with 25,000 men on board, it had originally planned to dock at Southampton, but was diverted to Plymouth because of German submarine activity in the Channel, and steamed into the Sound and then into the dockyard to let the men disembark. Three local cruisers, *Aboukir*, *Hogue* and *Cressey*, were sunk by a submarine off the Dutch coast and the battleship *Audacious* was lost on 27 October. The greatest early disaster for the town was the loss of *Monmouth*, a Devonport-manned ship, and *Cape of Good Hope* in the Battle of Coronel off the coast of Chile, against Admiral von Spee, fought on 1 November. Both ships went down with no survivors. A few days later the dreadnought cruisers *Invincible* and *Inflexible* arrived at Devonport to be fitted out, in record time, to take part in the battle of the Falkland Islands on 8 December, a major victory for the British fleet.

The Palace Theatre, Union Street, built in 1898.

The Battle of Jutland, fought in May 1916, resulted in a loss of fourteen ships to the Royal Navy, many of them Devonport-manned, and 6,274 men. One ship involved was the 26,000-ton battle cruiser *Lion*, flagship of Vice-Admiral Sir David Beatty. A Devonport-built vessel, manned by men from Devonport, it was badly damaged but saved from destruction by the heroic actions of turret officer Major F. Harvey, who ordered a magazine to be flooded. For this he was awarded a posthumous Victoria Cross. Other Devonport-built ships involved in the action at Jutland included *Minotaur*, *Temeraire, Collingwood, Indefatigable*, which was sunk with only two survivors, *Centurion*, and *Marlborough*, which returned to the Humber after being torpedoed.

The war in France was also responsible for many soldiers lost during the conflict, none more so than the Battle of the Bois des Buttes in May 1918, at which the 2nd Devon Regiment lost many men as well as their commander, Colonel Anderson-Morshead, scion of an old Plymouth merchant family. The names of the military personnel killed in action are remembered on the War Memorial erected after the war on the Hoe.

In June 1917 the Americans took over Victoria Wharf as a base and operated a large number of mass-produced submarine chasers. Within weeks two destroyers and over sixty submarine chasers were based there, with over 3,000 men working from the port and headquarters in Elliot Terrace. Many Q-ships, decoy vessels or armed merchant ships whose purpose was to lure submarines into surface attacks and then sink them, operated from Devonport, though their activities were kept a closely-guarded secret.

Early in the war a Royal Naval Air Service (RNAS) base was established at Chelson Meadow, known as RNAS Laira, a sub-station of the base at Mullion on the Lizard peninsula of Cornwall. The base was home to two airships, which were moored to the trees and painted in a camouflage khaki, brown and black. It is not clear when the area ceased to be used for military flights but the Chelson Meadow racecourse was certainly used by civilian flyers. Meanwhile, at the Cattewater a seaplane base had been established in September 1913 and several trial flights were made from it. In 1916 Mount Batten peninsula was closed to the public, and the RNAS set up a base in February 1917. Two hangars were erected close to the breakwater upon which a railway track was laid to enable a steam crane to move about lifting seaplanes into the water. Both the airship base and RNAS Cattewater came under the control of a large RNAS establishment at Tregantle, Cornwall, where Major-General Hutchison was in charge. At first the Castle Inn was used as the officers' mess, while the petty officers were in the coastguard cottages facing the Sound. Men were ferried across each day in the Oreston & Turnchapel Co.'s *Rapid*, until hangars and living quarters were built with slipways for the planes and motor launches attached.

On 1 April 1918 the RNAS merged with the Royal Flying Corps to become the Royal Air Force, and RAF Cattewater came into existence. The unit at Tregantle in Cornwall was closed and headquarters were transferred to Mount Wise Barracks, with Brigadier-General H.D. Briggs in command, and Mount Batten became an RAF station.

In 1918 most countries in the war-weary continent were suffering from the ravages of a severe influenza epidemic. By the end of July, thirty-five deaths had been reported in Plymouth, and during October and November the total figure was 432. Fortunately, by this time peace was approaching. On 11 November the massed sound from ships' sirens and whistles, joined by factories and warships in harbour, signalled to everyone that the conflict was over at last. One nine-year-old schoolboy, walking along College Road in Mutley that morning, was anxious he would be late for class until he heard

An aerial view of RAF Mount Batten and the Cattewater.

the sirens, arrived at school and found most of the pupils being sent home. A teacher patted him on the back and told him that there would be no lessons that day. Although there had not yet been any official announcement in the town, flags were being hung from windows as well as from the main buildings in the centre, and strings of bunting were hung across the roads in celebration. Church and school bells rang out at intervals, and continued to do so for the rest of the day. Crowds in their thousands congregated in New George Street outside the *Western Morning News* offices to wait for an official announcement to be published. At 11 a.m. news arrived from the Admiralty at Mount Wise, who had telephoned the newspaper staff which then placed an official notice in the window of their offices, and a formal proclamation was made by the mayor of Plymouth in Guildhall Square. As the scenes of rejoicing were taking place, two lorries of German prisoners of war passed by and had to halt because of the crowds. The prisoners looked pleased as they guessed what was happening, and everyone was magnanimous in showing restraint towards their former foe.

After the war was over and anti–U–boat patrols had ceased, the base at Mount Batten went into 'care and maintenance.' By April 1922 the one remaining squadron left was disbanded, and the base was turned over to a Care and Maintenance Unit. This was expected to be the end of the base but in 1923 the Cattewater Seaplane Station Bill was enacted and the base reopened on 1 October 1928 as RAF Mount Batten. Several seaplanes were stationed here over the years. In April 1935 Mount Batten became the Fleet Air Arm's floatplane base, under the command of Group-Captain I.T. Lloyd, with a total strength of twenty-three officers and 203 airmen. In October 1938 work began on constructing underground oil tanks at Radford Quarry for the use of RAF Mount Batten, and in January 1940 a pipeline was opened from Turnchapel Wharf to the tanks.

In peacetime the most pressing problem was the provision of new housing. Under the provisions of the 1919 Housing and Planning Act, which placed responsibility on local authorities to investigate housing problems and offered government help and grants to build new ones, a slum clearance programme began in Plymouth, with slum housing being gradually replaced. New council estates were started at Swilly, later renamed North Prospect, and by 1924 the Corporation had completed building 802 new council houses. The Great Western Railway built an estate for its workmen at Peverell and the Astors another at Mount Gould. The Admiralty also built new houses at St Budeaux to house men who had been displaced by the closure of Pembroke and Rosyth yards, the new road being appropriately named Pemros Road. The town had now expanded to the full extent of its official boundaries, and land for future development was severely limited. The population of the inner areas was declining, but that of the outer suburbs, especially Plympton and Plymstock, was growing rapidly. Plymstock alone had expanded from 7,032 in 1901 to 12,134 in 1931. By 1939 there were over 5,000 council flats and houses in Plymouth.

In the Liberal landslide General Election of 1906 both Plymouth Conservatives were defeated, though by the second election of 1910 the party had regained both seats, one of the new Members being Waldorf Astor. Among the Liberals elected between 1904 and 1910 was Sir John Benn, grandfather of the controversial late-twentieth-century Labour minister Tony Benn. One of the Conservatives elected for Devonport in 1910 was Sir John Jackson, who had been the contractor for a 114-acre extension to the dockyard in 1896, a scheme which cost some £6,000 and employed about 3,400 men. It was no surprise that the younger town's mainly working-class population tended to vote Liberal until the rise of Labour, and in 1912 the secretary of Devonport Labour Party spoke despondently of an electorate 'largely swayed by "Big Navyism".'

After political reorganisation in 1918 Plymouth returned three Members to Parliament, for the constituencies of Devonport, Sutton and Drake. Waldorf Astor had represented Sutton since 1910 until his father's death in October 1919 when he was elevated to the peerage. By resigning his seat in the House of Commons, he caused a by-election in November in which his wife, Nancy, stood as Coalition Unionist (in effect Conservative) candidate. There was no little prejudice against the candidature of a woman, and when she won the contest with a victory of 5,203 over the Labour candidate she achieved a historic feat, becoming the first woman to take her seat at Westminster. With her outgoing personality and ready wit, she was more than a match for any heckler on the hustings. When someone shouted at her, 'You're too rich to get the working man's vote,' she retorted, 'You'll see. It won't be the 17,000 millionaires living on the Hoe who will elect me.' Having had an alcoholic ex-husband and a similarly afflicted son by her first brief marriage, she was passionately opposed throughout her parliamentary career to any liberalisation of the licensing laws. To the present day, housing estates in Plymouth which were built on land previously owned by the Astor family still have no public houses, because of covenants in the original deeds.

Lady Nancy Astor,
1925.

In October 1928, on the recommendation of the Home Secretary, the County Borough of Plymouth was granted city status by King George V, and a tablet to commemorate the event was placed in the northern wall of the Guildhall. To celebrate the King's Silver Jubilee, on 6 May 1935 it received a second charter and the Chief Magistrate was granted the right to use the style and title of Lord Mayor. A proclamation was read out by the town clerk at a ceremony on 9 May in the Guildhall Square, after which the Lord Mayor, Alderman Pillar, his deputy and their wives then went into the Council Chamber for a special council meeting. The private residence of Lord and Lady Astor, No. 3 Eliot Terrace, on the Hoe, was presented some years later by Lady Astor to the City of Plymouth as a residence for future Lord Mayors and used for civic hospitality by visiting dignitaries and High Court judges.

Among the Astors' friends who enjoyed their hospitality was the iconoclastic playwright George Bernard Shaw. When Lord and Lady Astor presented a Hall of

Residence at the Manor Lodge, Devonport, the Astor Hall, they invited Shaw to give an address at the opening in October 1929. He accepted the invitation, delivering an address to a crowded Devonport Guildhall which included some typically eccentric and tongue-in-cheek remarks. 'The extraordinary devotion of my friends Lord and Lady Astor to the City of Plymouth has always been a source of astonishment to me,' he started, 'because I have never been able to understand in what way the citizens of Plymouth have ever deserved it.' He then said that English university education was destroying civilisation, and for centuries had been making decent government and life for the people impossible. After he had sat down, Lady Astor thanked him and said that there were few people who could speak as he did – and perhaps it was as well for the world that there were.

Other well-known friends of the Astors paid visits to Plymouth at around this time. The most flamboyant was King George V's cousin Queen Marie of Romania, eldest daughter of Alfred, Duke of Edinburgh. As a girl she had lived at Admiralty House during his tenure of office as Commander-in-Chief, and she spent a few days in the area in May 1924, staying at Eliot Terrace and visiting Cotehele, Mount Edgcumbe and Devonport. Another was Aircraftman T.E. Shaw, who worked at Mount Batten between February 1929 and 1933 as general orderly for the flight commanders, and also designed the squadron's crest, based on a photograph he took of a cormorant with wings outstretched standing on a mooring buoy. Shaw was better known as 'Lawrence of Arabia', and had come to Plymouth to work under an alias as he was embarrassed by the semi-legendary status his role in the Middle East during the war had brought him.

Another *History of Plymouth* was published in 1931. The author, C.W. (Charles William) Bracken, had been headmaster of Plymouth Corporation Grammar School from 1909 until retiring in 1930. His work appeared in an updated edition with a postscript published in 1970, twenty years after his death. It was an inspiration to two historians of the next generation. The first was R.A.J. (Robert Alfred John) Walling, whose career also included a spell as Chairman of the Bench, Plymouth Magistrates' Court, Managing Editor of the Western Newspaper Co., and editor of the *Western Independent*, Plymouth's Sunday newspaper, as well as author of other books about the West Country and over twenty thrillers. He died a few months before the publication of *The Story of Plymouth* in 1950. The second was one of Bracken's pupils, Crispin Gill, whose *Plymouth: A New History* was first published in two parts in 1966 and 1979 and then in a revised one-volume edition in 1993.

The Corporation centralised its garaging at the Milehouse depot and bought its first buses in 1920 to serve areas not properly catered for by the tram network. Buses gradually replaced trams, and in 1939 the Peverell route was the only one left where the latter still ran. Private bus companies were set up just after the war, using buses rebuilt on army lorry chasses. The first major private firm was the Embankment Motor Co., followed by the Devon Motor Transport Co. There was much competition in the form of fare-cutting between both firms, until the Devon Motor Transport Co. was taken over by the National Bus Co., which operated the first double-decker buses. In 1929 the GWR acquired a controlling interest in road transport and formed the Western National Bus Co.

One of Plymouth's great landmarks of the inter-war years was the Tinside Lido. A scheme had been put forward in 1913 for bathing facilities at Tinside Beach on the Hoe, and the bathing houses were formally opened in August that year. Further developments took place a few years later with the erection of limestone-fronted bathing houses and terraces on the western ends of the bay, the building of the higher terraces, the bridge and new dressing rooms, which were opened in June 1930. Further facilities, including the cliff paths and promenade, sun-bathing terraces, steps from Madeira Road, a concreted foreshore to enable young children to go paddling, a diving chute, the rafts, a protection groyne on the western end of the bay, a new approach to the eastern foreshore, public conveniences, a circular extension to an existing groyne which would allow bathers to enter the water at low tides, a trial of floodlit bathing and the subsequent installation of electric lighting, completed the venture. Though it fell into disuse in the 1980s it became a Grade II Listed Building in 1998, to be redeveloped and reopened in August 2003.

During the Great Depression of the 1920s, in common with many other industries the dockyard had to lay off members of its workforce. Plymouth had always relied heavily on the dockyard for employment, and it was said locally that when the yard caught a cold, the town always sneezed. From its wartime peak of nearly 19,000 the labour force fell steadily to 11,436 in 1925 and 10,854 in 1927. Immediately after the war the more newly-recruited and temporary staff had been the first to go, but by 1924 redundancies were affecting more and more men who had assumed they had a job for life. Several strikes disrupted civilian industry, including a dockers' strike in 1919 which held up coal supplies and came close to leaving the town without gas, and a builders' strike which lasted six weeks. During the General Strike in 1926, strikers played a friendly football match with the police at Home Park on 8 May, the strikers winning 2-1. Nevertheless relations between the public and those taking industrial action were less harmonious elsewhere in the town, and in some quarters feelings ran so high that trams rumbling through the streets had to be covered in wire netting to reduce damage and personal injury should they be pelted with stones and other missiles. During the match, 4,000 strikers and their supporters were hurling sticks and rocks at the police and at volunteer drivers, to try and stop them moving trams from Drake Circus to the town centre.

The Labour Party found converts ready to rally under the leadership of Jimmy Moses, leader of the Shipwrights' Union. Dartmouth-born Moses had been elected to Devonport Borough Council in 1911, where he was a fervent supporter of amalgamation in 1914, and became an alderman in 1921. When he left the Liberal Party to join Labour in 1918 several of his supporters followed him, and in 1926 he was elected first Labour Mayor of Plymouth. In the General Election of 1929 he was elected Member of Parliament for the Drake division, becoming the town's first Labour Member, although he was defeated in 1931.

The 1929 election saw each of the three major parties represented for one of the Plymouth constituencies. Leslie Hore-Belisha had first won Devonport as a Liberal in 1923; as a Member of the National Government from 1931 he was Secretary of State for Transport from 1934 and then for War from 1937. Nancy Astor, a passionate fighter for local interests, held Sutton for the Conservatives for twenty-five years, though in 1929 it was a closely-fought contest and she only won by a majority of 211 votes over the Labour candidate after a re-count.

Despite the economic downturn of the 1920s, Plymouth continued to flourish commercially, and as the largest urban centre in England west of Bristol established itself as the chief entertainment and shopping centre for Devon and Cornwall. The major stores, including Spooner's, Popham's, Yeo's and Dingle's, all opened premises in the town centre, which stretched from Drake's Circus to Derry's Clock. Devonport's own

Jimmy Moses, Plymouth's first Labour Mayor in 1926 and first Labour
Member of Parliament (for the Drake constituency) in 1929.

shopping centre could not compete, and declined accordingly. The Hoe Pier was the main
venue of touring concert parties, and people strolling along the promenade on summer
evenings would always hear much singing and dancing. At the turn of the century the
Palace Theatre of Varieties, the Royal and Grand Theatres, all played to packed houses,
but in the 1920s they gradually lost most of their audiences as cinema-going increased in
popularity. A picture house was built in Union Street, then the Cinedrome in Ebrington
Street, formerly a skating rink, was turned into the New Palladium, and the Regent and
Gaumont cinemas were built. Theatre audiences declined dramatically, and in 1938 the
Royal Theatre was replaced by a 2,400-seater cinema.

Plymouth Pier, *c.* 1910.

Plymouth Pier with Drake's Island in the background. (Courtesy of M. Richards)

At the turn of the century Plymouth had three daily papers, two morning and one evening. All were purchased by Sir Leicester Harmsworth, brother of the press barons Lord Northcliffe and Lord Rothermere. The *Western Daily Mercury* had never shown a profit during its sixty-year existence, and in 1921 it was amalgamated with the *Western Morning News*, while the *Western Evening Herald* was published from the same office.

Plymouth Argyle Football Club, founded in 1885, was a major attraction, drawing in faithful crowds whether it was going up or down in the Third and Second Divisions of the Football League. Its home ground was Home Park, built and opened in 1893. The club had gained entry to the Southern League in 1903 following exhibition matches against several other major national teams, joined the football league in 1920, and reached the Second Division in 1930. Matches regularly attracted crowds of 20,000 or more, with big fixtures often attracting up to 40,000. In 1936 a record 43,596 fans crowded into the park for a visit by Aston Villa from Birmingham. From Penzance shoppers could take a 5s fortnightly train to coincide with Plymouth Argyle's home games, and this would bring between 2,500 and 3,000 people to Plymouth each time. Similar excursions to Plymouth were run from other towns in Devon and Cornwall.

By the late 1930s employment in the dockyard was rising, though Plymouth's unemployment rate was above the national average. The liner trade was still thriving, with up to 40,000 passengers per annum passing through the port, in addition to a large number of mail bags. The Cunard liners *Aquitania*, *Mauretania* and *Queen Mary* were frequent visitors. Fishing, which had been one of Plymouth's most important industries for several hundred years, continued to play a role in the region's prosperity; fish harvests were usually good, and boats working out of Sutton Harbour did well.

As ever the city still needed room for expansion. Its boundaries were extended in 1938 to include the remainder of St Budeaux parish, thus growing from 5,711 acres to 9,595 acres, a net increase of 68 per cent. The northern boundary now extended from Budshead Creek to the main Plymouth to Tavistock road.

The renewed threat of military action from Germany had resulted in a rearmament programme and subsequent build-up of the dockyard, with many more men being taken on in the workforce. Plymouth had an unpleasant foretaste of the possible shape of things to come with the creation of a local branch of Oswald Mosley's British Union of Fascists. Their meetings were rowdy affairs, and when a crowd of about 4,000 came to hear a speech from Mosley in Millbay Drillhall on 5 October 1934, the proceedings ended in a brawl. A press photographer and a *Western Morning News* reporter were verbally attacked and physically abused, and the former had his camera destroyed. The paper henceforth declared that it would no longer provide the movement with any publicity unless 'some adequate explanation and reparation' was forthcoming. Moreover, there were internal differences with disagreement between the Plymouth Fascists and the Blackshirts from London on the use of violence by people from Mosley's men in London. Local membership of the party soon dwindled to a rump, and the organisation's local office in Lockyer Street closed down in 1935.

Three years later a warning was issued by Admiral Sir Reginald Plunkett-Ernle-Erle-Drax, who was appointed Commander-in-Chief at Mount Wise in 1935. Shortly before his tenure of office ended in October 1938 he spoke at a dinner attended by the Lord Mayor and about 200 naval officers, warning of the likelihood of war and the country's need to be prepared for such an eventuality. As he had served in the Royal Navy during the First World War at Jutland and other naval battles, he knew well that it did not pay to underestimate the enemy. As Devonport's Member of Parliament and Minister for War, Leslie Hore-Belisha

Old Town Street, 1889. (Courtesy of M. Richards)

Old Town Street before the German air raids of the Second World War.
(Courtesy of M. Richards)

was responsible for modernising the armed forces and creating anti-aircraft defences in
order to face the threat from abroad, and he found it necessary to reintroduce conscription
in the face of strong opposition from the then Prime Minister, Neville Chamberlain.

By 1939 Plymouth had a population of about 225,000. Some of the wealthier
residents had recently moved from the city to more salubrious areas such as Plymstock
and Plympton, which were just outside the boundaries. A quarter of a century after
the amalgamation of the three towns, its central streets and shopping areas remained
largely as they had been at the end of the Victorian age. The atmosphere was one of a
small market town, already beginning to experience gridlock in the streets as a result
of rising car ownership. Heavy traffic was an increasing problem, and Spooner's Corner,
at the junction of Bedford Street and Old Town Street, had the unenviable reputation
of being the most congested corner in the country outside London. Significant
replanning was a priority, but nobody could foresee just how much imminent events
would force the pace of change in Plymouth.

eight

Plymouth in the Second World War

On Sunday 3 September 1939, an eighty-strong congregation attended morning service at St Augustine's Church, Lipson Vale. As Mr Clemmer, the sidesman, presented the collection plate, he whispered to the vicar that war had just been declared on Germany. After a short silence they sang the hymn 'Breathe on me, Breath of God,' while the worshippers knelt in prayer, then the vicar made a short statement about the news.

The outbreak of war was viewed in Plymouth with mixed feelings. All those who were old enough to remember the earlier conflict just over two decades before were well aware that any major military hostilities would mean the loss of able-bodied men leaving home to fight, many never to return. However, Plymouth itself had had the good fortune to remain otherwise relatively unscathed between 1914 and 1918, with no structural damage as a result of enemy action, and there was little reason to suppose that the situation would be different this time. Additionally, for those who were unemployed it meant new hope with a full dockyard, more hands required for armament purposes as well as building and repairing warships, and for retailers there would doubtless be an influx of servicemen to bring spending money into the town. If imminent events were to follow a similar pattern to that of the First World War, some thought such a state of affairs would probably be to Plymouth's advantage. Few had any idea of just how devastating for the city the next few years were going to be.

Within a few weeks, the authorities in Plymouth began to prepare for the worst by rehearsing methods of dealing with attack from the air. An Emergency Committee consisting of the three party leaders was set up and the town clerk, Colin Campbell, was appointed Air Raid Precautions Officer. Anti-aircraft batteries were established, barrage balloons were developed, and air-raid sirens were put under single remote control at Greenbank Police Headquarters. Among precautions taken was a warning on public noticeboards that children were not permitted to imitate the warning signal of the air-raid siren. With the call-up and able-bodied young men joining the services, shop staff were depleted by an average of 25 per cent. Dingles restricted its deliveries, and country customers were served by horse-drawn vehicles.

With so many planes and squadrons at RAF Mount Batten, the base became so crowded that the Fleet Air Arm had to move back to Lee-on-Solent. By the outbreak of the Second World War there was a squadron of Sunderland flying boats stationed at Mount Batten, which patrolled the south-western approaches in partnership with the two squadrons at Pembroke Dock in Pembrokeshire. On 9 September 1939 a Sunderland launched the first attack on a German U-boat in the Channel and on 18 September another helped to rescue the crew off the SS *Kensington Court*, which had been torpedoed about seventy miles off the Isles of Scilly. The Sunderland's pilot, Flight-Lieutenant Barrett, dropped eight of his bombs on the spot where the U-boat had been submerged before he was able to land and pick up fourteen of the crew from the stricken cargo vessel. Every member of the crew was saved, and Barrett was awarded the Distinguished Flying Cross.

When 204 Squadron left for North Africa it was replaced on 1 April 1940 by Number 10 Royal Australian Air Force Squadron, who stayed at Plymouth for the duration of the war, leaving the base in October 1945. By then its members had flown 4,553,860 nautical miles, undertaken 3,177 operational flights, and sunk five submarines. Before they left England they were awarded a Crest by King George VI with the motto 'Strike First'.

On 30 January 1940 HMS *Ajax* sailed into Plymouth Sound under cover of darkness after seeing action against the pocket battleship *Graf Spee* in the Battle of the River Plate, Argentina, and was given a rapturous welcome when word spread. On 15 February HMS *Exeter*, built in Devonport and carrying a largely local crew, returned from the same theatre of war, having suffered serious damage. It came back to a welcome from Winston Churchill, First Lord of the Admiralty, who came on board before it docked. The officers and men from both ships were given a civic reception in the Guildhall on 16 February. After a refit in Devonport, *Exeter* joined the First Cruiser Squadron in the Home Fleet, and later saw service in the Middle East. On 1 March 1942 it was scuttled by the crew after action against overwhelming Japanese forces in the Dutch East Indies, during which fifty-four officers and men were lost.

Not until the Germans reached the English Channel in the summer of 1940 was the 'phoney war' over, and only then did Plymouth seriously consider how vulnerable it could be to enemy action. On 2 June a contingent of French troops, newly evacuated from Dunkirk, arrived at Turnchapel station to await re-embarkation for France. The need to offer them appropriate hospitality placed some pressure on the city's resources, but such was the state of organisation that within a day or so of the men's arrival a canteen service was being provided in the docks, while people all over the city were ready to volunteer help by offering sleeping accommodation and baths. Just over two weeks later, at 5.30 p.m. on 18 June, the ex-Great Western Railway Channel Islands ferry *St Helier* anchored in Plymouth Sound, after diverting while on passage from Southampton to La Pallice on the French coast. When it sailed again later that evening to resume its mission, the captain was surprised to pass French ships of all types making haste for the English ports. The situation on land was deteriorating and shortly afterwards *St Helier* was attacked by two enemy planes. The crew replied with heavy fire from the ship's guns and scored hits on both planes, causing a bomb which had been intended for the ship to fall some way short. Aware that any attempt to embark troops would almost certainly end in disaster, the ship was ordered to sea, where it ran the gauntlet of an enemy submarine and a severe electrical storm. It finally arrived back in the relative safety of Plymouth Sound on 21 June.

A few days later, on 30 June, the first siren alarm of the war sounded and the population made their way to the nearest shelter. It proved to be a false alarm. A second came on the morning of 4 July, the first to occur during the school day. The headmaster of Johnston Terrace School noted in the school's log book that the children went to the shelter at 10.30 a.m. and stayed there for an hour, during which time they behaved very well.

Nevertheless, during the next four years sirens would sound at Plymouth over 400 times, and there would be fifty-nine bombing raids. The first of these came just before

Derry's Clock during the Blitz.

midday on 6 July 1940, when three bombs hit a block of eight houses on a housing estate at Swilly Road, Devonport, resulting in the destruction of three houses and severe damage to several nearby properties. Three people − a man, a woman and a boy − were killed, and six others were injured. Nevertheless children from London and the cities of the Midlands were being evacuated to Plymouth at this time, and as yet the authorities at Whitehall saw no need to send anyone out of the city. It was a source of bitterness for some time, even after the war, that while local councillors and organisations were pressing for children to be sent away from the area as part of a carefully organised evacuation scheme, the powers in London were slow to act and did not consider it a priority until enemy action was at its worst the following year.

On the afternoon of 7 July in a second raid, planes flew down the Plym Valley. One plane came so low that a man on duty at the gasworks at Coxside, which were evidently the target, fired at it with a shotgun but missed. It landed on houses at the junction of South Milton Street and Home Sweet Home Terrace, killing five people and injuring four, one of whom died in hospital a few days later, and the post office was destroyed. Next morning four bombs were dropped in the area of Morice Square and Marlborough Street, Devonport. A butcher was killed when his shop was hit, and three others were seriously injured. These raids continued for the next few weeks, often aimed at selective targets including RAF Mount Batten, the dockyard, North Road Station, and public utilities such as the gas and electricity works. Several houses were destroyed in Goschen Street and Hamilton Street, Keyham Barton, in an afternoon raid on 25 August, and two days later another raid killed twelve patients and staff at Ford Residential House home in Wolseley Road.

Families then began to leave Plymouth for the safer towns and villages of Devon and Cornwall. This evacuation later became official, and at one stage the population fell from 220,000 in 1939 to 127,000. Arrangements for emergency feeding and housing

Marlborough Street after the Blitz, 1941.

were hastily made, but ironically most of the premises which had been designated thus were close to target areas and therefore frequently destroyed or damaged themselves, meaning somewhere else had to be found quickly. The War Office in Whitehall gave little assistance, apparently reluctant to acknowledge that Plymouth was at risk, despite the strategic importance of the dockyard and its status as the largest city west of Bristol. Local government was inevitably hampered by the loss of records and the repeated destruction of offices, and enlistment depleted the number of civic employees. Early protection facilities for the general public were inadequate, while many of the early shelters were small and easily flooded. Anderson shelters were made free to households who had an income of less than £250 per year, and later Morrison shelters were also made available.

At the outbreak of war G.S. Scoble, a Labour Member of the city council, was Lord Mayor. He completed his term of office on 9 November 1939, and the leaders of all three parties wanted his successor to be someone who would personify unity at the head of local affairs. The unanimous choice was Lord Astor. Although a lifelong Conservative he was on the progressive wing of the party, and shared to a degree the Labour Party's vision of comprehensive long-term planning in urban and rural areas. He agreed to serve in that capacity for the duration of the war, and worked continuously within the city for the war effort. Within a week of taking office, he realised that it would be pointless to have many different appeals for local charities all competing with each other. Instead, he decided, there should be a single one, the Lord Mayor's Fund, administered by a representative committee which would receive and consider every application for worthy causes. To help raise money he proposed a covenant by which people would be encouraged to subscribe a certain sum each week or month, while groups of people in societies, offices, schools, factories, stores and workshops were asked to appoint officers to collect and forward their regular contributions. Before long the Fund was raising money at the rate of £10,000 per year. When Neville Chamberlain resigned as Prime Minister in May 1940 and Churchill succeeded him, Astor was offered a post in the wartime government as Minister of Agriculture because of his commitment to the gradual nationalisation of agricultural land, but he declined it on the grounds that his first duty was to the people of Plymouth.

The bombs gradually increased in size, with new landmines being dropped by parachute. The first incendiary attack came on 28 November 1940 when an enemy aircraft dropped four flares over the Turnchapel and Mount Batten district, and several thousand landmines, as well as a large number of bombs. Almost at once one of the hangars at RAF Mount Batten was set alight by a high explosive bomb, and a Sunderland flying boat was destroyed. Within a short while another bomber, while aiming for the Air Station, achieved a direct hit on an oil tank in the nearby Admiralty Oil Fuel Depot, adjacent to Turnchapel railway station, starting a major conflagration. At Oreston ten people were killed, and four houses were demolished. As the fires around the tanks continued into the next day, two men from the Auxiliary Fire Service were killed and four others were injured. An explosion resulted in a shower of blazing oil on the railway station, and the adjacent buildings immediately caught fire. The flames burnt fiercely until they were finally put out on 1 December. Throughout Plymouth, everyone went in dread of further indiscriminate bombing attacks in any area of the city, and there was a mass evacuation from Turnchapel to Plympton.

About a hundred planes had taken part in the raid. The first incendiaries were reasonably small and could be kept under control to some extent with water and sand from individuals, but the later explosive and non-explosive types included delayed firing devices that still burnt while being tackled. Both the Plymouth and Stonehouse Gas Co. and the Plymouth Corporation Electricity Works were hit during one attack, and for a brief period Plymouth had no electrical power anywhere in the city. Local gas supplies were vulnerable to persistent disruption, and there were a number of tragic accidents in the course of repair work. Hundreds of houses were destroyed, and the Emergency Committee had the additional responsibility of feeding and housing the homeless. The council provided food and shelter for two days, and after that people were billeted in private houses, with an allowance of 5s for each adult and 3s for each child to the hosts.

On 20 March 1941 King George VI and Queen Elizabeth, and the Australian Prime Minister, Robert Menzies, paid a visit to Plymouth. The King inspected Civil Defence and Home Guard units, and talked to many local people. As the Queen remarked to a warden, 'it is only by keeping our chins up, as we are doing, that we shall win the war.' They left on the royal train from Millbay at about 5.30 p.m. Meanwhile, that day rumours had been circulating around the Royal Air Force operational room at St Eval, Cornwall, that Plymouth 'was due to catch a packet tonight.' In preparation, they made ready four Gloster Gladiator biplanes for the defence of the city.

Three hours after the royal train left the city the alert sounded, and at 8.39 p.m. an attack started from a group of Heinkel III bombers flying at between 9,900ft and 11,500ft. Included in the bombs that they dropped were thirty-four delayed-action high-explosive ones. The pathfinder force, which should have arrived first and dropped flares to light the target, arrived at 8.41 p.m., flying at an altitude of 19,000ft. Their shower of flares was followed by 12,500 incendiaries and other high-explosive bombs. Once they had turned away to go back home to their airfields in France, two further squadrons dropped their bomb loads, which included seventeen blockbusters. In addition, a squadron that had been sent to bomb the Westland Aircraft factory,

Yeovil, diverted to direct bombs on Plymouth when bad weather prevented them from finding their original target.

During this raid Spooners premises, across the road from St Andrew's Church, were the first to suffer. The flames were spreading so fast that the city's own fire brigade was unable to contain the situation. Within thirty minutes an urgent call went out to other fire brigades all over the West Country asking for help, and this was soon extended to places as far away as Birmingham, Swindon and Salisbury. Next to suffer were the Royal Hotel and the general post office in Westwell Street which were destroyed, and the Municipal Offices which sustained some damage. The illumination from these fires made it easier for a second wave of planes to bomb an area of the town extending almost from Stonehouse to Mutley and Cattedown.

Between then and 11.30 p.m. some 125 enemy aircraft brought terror to the city, and by around midnight the centre of Plymouth was aflame. When the other fire brigades arrived, their sole navigational aid being the bright orange glow in the night sky which indicated where Plymouth was, they found they could only be of limited help with putting out fires because their equipment was not compatible with that already being used in the city. They had to rely mostly on the ordinary water mains. As one fireman remarked, it was 'like trying to put out a blazing warehouse with a stirrup-pump,' and many of the fires had to be left to burn themselves out. That night alone 336 people were killed.

The city centre was extensively damaged, and the carnage inflicted the following night, 21 March, was even worse, with heat from the fires being so extensive that plate glass melted and asphalt roadways turned to liquid. At about 8.50 p.m. it started once again without warning, when the sudden appearance of raiders coming in from the north-east caught the city by surprise. This time the target was the area adjoining the one hit the previous night, and pathfinder planes encircled Plymouth for about twenty minutes as they positioned themselves before dropping their flares on the chosen spot. Bombers soon followed, and encountered almost no resistance from the Royal Air Force. Fires soon ranged over a wide region, from the timber yards and tar distillery at Coxside in the east, to the Royal Naval Barracks at Keyham and the Royal William Victualling Yard in the west. One man was killed and two were injured on Drake's Island. St Andrew's Church, the Guildhall and the Municipal Offices, which had all been fortunate to escape the previous night, were gutted. The Westminster and Hacker's Hotels in the Crescent, and the Plymouth Co-operative store, were razed to the ground. A bomb at the Royal Naval Barracks destroyed a petty officers' block, killing eighty people, while a large underground shelter in Portland Square suffered a direct hit and seventy-two people were killed. Milehouse bus depot was almost obliterated; one complete bus was thrown onto the roof of the main shed, and fifty buses were destroyed. Derry's Clock Tower remained standing, but the faces of the clock were broken by flying debris.

Many churches were burnt out, including King Street Wesleyan Church and the Baptist Church in George Street (the shell of Charles Church has been preserved ever since as a memorial to those who lost their lives). The Hoe Pier, Hoe Café and Hoe Grammar School, the Prince of Wales Hospital and the Royal Sailors' Rest all suffered a similar fate. Five servicemen were killed at Osborne Place, the Hoe, by an unexploded bomb. As there was no city centre left for the buses to serve, the Western National Omnibus Co. moved its terminus from St Andrew's Cross to Sherwell Arcade, close to the City Museum in Tavistock Road.

St Andrew's Church after the Blitz, 1941.

By the morning of 22 March, the only buildings still undamaged in the city centre were the Westminster Bank in Bedford Street and the *Western Morning News* office in Frankfort Street. Providentially, both buildings had been constructed only a few years earlier from fire-resistant materials. The newspaper's storage area which housed the photographic collection was however destroyed, resulting in the loss to posterity of a unique photographic archive which comprised thousands of irreplaceable prints and negatives of old Plymouth.

Further raids came in April, bringing the death toll in March and April 1941 to 926. The worst of these was on the night of 22 April, resulting in the destruction of the Air Raid Precaution's control centre beneath Devonport Market and an attack on Devonport Telephone Exchange. Devonport had been a target because of the dockyard, and its shopping centre was virtually gone. Only two badly damaged stores, Marks & Spencer and Burton's, were left standing, and what was left of them was eventually razed to the ground in favour of dockyard extensions.

In another raid, some 72,000 books were destroyed in a fire at the Central Library in Tavistock Road, including 41,000 in the lending library, 16,000 in the reference department and the Devon and Cornwall Collection of 15,000 books. Fortunately 5,000 were out on loan and therefore saved. Some stock was salvaged, but it was mainly thanks to the general public donating 4,500 books and Isaac Foot also generously presenting several thousand from his own library that the service was able to start again quickly after such a disaster. On 8 August the Lord Mayor reopened the lending library on a temporary basis in the museum part of the building, which had miraculously remained unscathed. When the BBC announced that morning that the raid had been 'short and sharp,' they were forced to amend the statement.

Plymouth city centre after the Blitz, 1941.

Naval ratings from HMS *Raleigh* at Torpoint were given the job of recovering bodies from the ruins. The victims of the April air raids were buried in a mass grave at Efford cemetery on the afternoon of 28 April, each coffin draped with a Union Flag and floral tributes ranging from humble posies of primroses to official wreaths and crosses. Those taking part in the service included the Bishop of Exeter, the Bishop of Plymouth, the Roman Catholic Bishop of Plymouth and the Revd W.D. Campbell representing the Nonconformist congregations. Representatives from the Salvation Army and officers from the armed services also attended. A fighter airfield constructed at Yelverton, using large amounts of rubble from the destruction of Plymouth for its runways, was open by 15 August 1941. Groups of servicemen were sent to help salvage stock from bombed shop premises. They entered each damaged shop in turn, reclaiming everything worth salvaging and laying it out on tarpaulin sheets for owners to examine what had been saved and assess what had been destroyed.

While Plymouth was recovering from the worst of the war damage, the city centre was cordoned off. Main roads were guarded by armed soldiers and policemen, and soldiers were also stationed in railway signal boxes. The object was to prevent the place from spectators from Devon and Cornwall who evidently had nothing better to do than to come and see the ruins as if they were some kind of tourist attraction. Those who came to look before the cordon was in place caused considerable resentment amongst those who had suffered.

Double summer time was introduced on 4 May 1941, thus putting the United Kingdom two hours ahead of Greenwich Mean Time. This had the effect of shortening Plymouth's blackout period and giving an extra hour of daylight for clearing-up operations on the city streets which were strewn with glass, timber and debris, and riddled with bomb craters. Tradesmen making deliveries in motor vehicles were regularly experiencing punctures.

By the first week of May 1941, seventy-one Plymouth fire-fighters were on the sick list, mostly through exhaustion. Arrangements were made to bring in an extra hundred firemen from Wales as a temporary measure. Many civil defence workers also needed a sustained period of rest, and an exchange of civil defence personnel was arranged with others outside Plymouth to allow them a break.

As Member of Parliament for Sutton, Lady Astor fought hard to obtain official recognition of Plymouth's plight and government help for the city. She was particularly angry that the House of Commons only debated the Fire Services (Emergency Provisions) Bill later in May, after Plymouth had been devastated by enemy action over several weeks. During the Blitz she became famous for raising morale among the city's servicemen and civilians by performing cartwheels to entertain sailors, and leading regular dances on the Hoe.

On 10 October 1941 a parade of tanks left Mutley Plain for the Octagon, where they went on show to raise funds under the banner of 'Speed the Tanks'. The 25-ton *Waltzing Matilda* and the two 16-ton *Valentine* tanks plus scout cars and breakdown lorries, under the command of Lt F.J. Turpin, appealed to the public 'for all the tanks you can give both ourselves and the Russians.' Three months later, in accordance with the provisions of the Emergency Powers (Defence) Acts of 1939 and 1940, a start was made in the Mutley area with the collection of what were deemed the city's least essential railings for iron and steel scrap, though any considered to be of particular historical or ornamental interest would be spared. Owners of properties thus affected were invited to claim for compensation, and collection was extended to Compton, Crownhill, St Budeaux, Pennycross and Molesworth wards about a week later.

The city council took over disused bakeries in Commercial Road and Treville Street in order to provide cooked meals to residents made homeless as a result of the bombing, with retired naval cooks and unemployed bakers providing the service at a rate of 1s 3½d per hour, plus a war bonus of 6s per week and double pay on Sundays. 'Blitz Soup,' comprising beans, lentils, peas, carrots and macaroni, was served in restaurants throughout the city. Though cinemas remained open, the available refreshments were curtailed. From September 1942, patrons could no longer buy ice creams during the interval, a restriction which remained in force until March 1945, while the sale of chocolates was likewise withdrawn a few months later.

About twice the amount of housing stock that existed before the war was destroyed during it as a consequence of rebuilt houses being successively hit. Although the dockyards were the principal targets, civilian casualties were high. Looting of bombed houses was frequent. On any night that a raid was expected tens of thousands trekked out into the countryside, usually onto the fringes of Dartmoor. Some owners of large properties in the countryside near Plymouth charged exorbitant rents to evacuees, and even families who made their way to the edge of the moor each night were charged for sleeping in cowsheds.

Despite severe damage to the city, efforts were made to try and keep up some spirit of normality. Some of the larger stores, including Dingles, Spooners, Yeos and Pophams, moved to small, older makeshift shops on the edge of the centre, and many open-air stalls were erected. Mutley Plain had escaped damage, and as the stores' main refuge, for a time it became the city's only shopping area of any size. The retail industry had been the city's second largest employer before 1939. Loss of staff and a fall in the population, and therefore customers, added to the woes of shops trying to recover from the loss of their premises and much of their stock.

Winston and Clementine Churchill in Plymouth, May 1941.

After a raid on 28 April, Mr A. Titherley, senior regional officer of the Ministry of Health, met the city's Emergency Committee and agreed that a large part of Plymouth should be declared an evacuation area, but only certain areas were to be scheduled for moving people away at first. For several weeks before, local officials had operated an evening evacuation. Winston Churchill, the Prime Minster, visited Plymouth on 2 May and toured the blitzed areas. As Lord Astor was ill, he was met and entertained by Lady Astor. There was a temporary lifting of morale, though no lasting improvements were seen.

On 3 March 1942 a number of City of Plymouth police and fire officers attended an investiture at Buckingham Palace, where King George VI presented them with the British Empire Medal for their bravery and gallant conduct during the heavy bombing raids of the previous year. On 20 March, around the first anniversary of the large air raids, King Peter of Yugoslavia arrived in Plymouth, and took the salute the following day at the Plymouth Warship Week parade. On 23 April a gilt silver cup given to Sir Francis Drake by Queen Elizabeth I was bought at Christie's in London by the National Arts Collection for £2,100, and it was announced that the cup was to be presented to the City of Plymouth in recognition of the gallantry of its inhabitants. During a three-day tour of Devon and Cornwall the King and Queen made a surprise visit to Plymouth on 7 May.

Plymouth became an officially protected area, and a stringent watch was kept for enemy aliens. A 9.30 every night a curfew for transport was imposed, with theatres and cinemas having to close by 9 p.m. Public houses remained open until 10 p.m., but customers who insisted on remaining until closing time generally had to walk home afterwards. Before the war Plymouth had decided to scrap the tram routes, but some tracks still remained in place, especially on the Peverell route, and any trams still available were brought back into use. All possible space was used for growing food. Part of the Hoe was dug up, ploughed and tilled by the Corporation gardeners so that vegetables could be grown there. A Corporation piggery was created in the old farm at Central Park, with the pigs being fed on kitchen scraps placed in refuse bins by the public.

National League football was suspended and the grass grew high on the untended pitch. The Plymouth Argyle stands were bombed in 1941, but local football was kept alive with the formation of the Plymouth City Club and the Plymouth United Club, who played games against service teams. Greyhound racing was a major attraction at Plymouth Greyhound Stadium. Both local newspapers, *Western Morning News* and *Western Evening Herald*, continued to publish six days a week, though for a while the nightly disruption meant that the *Western Morning News* had to be printed at the offices of the *Express & Echo* in Exeter until offices at Tavistock could be made available for the purpose. Production was based there until October 1944, when staff returned to the Plymouth office.

Pat Twyford, a war correspondent on the editorial staff of the paper, and later author of *It Came to our Door*, a detailed account of the city's wartime experiences, was involved in regular wartime journeys to Exeter. He later painted an evocative portrait in words of 'the fearful picture' of the city as he and his colleagues left 'the inferno' behind them, him driving while they looked back, 'watching that terrible glow in the sky which marked the burning city.' The *Western Evening Herald* maintained production in Frankfort Street as the work could be carried out during daytime, when raids were less likely to occur. One unsavoury headline, a sign of the times, came in November 1942 when a twenty-one-year-old Plymouth-born merchant seaman, Duncan Alexander Scott-Ford, was convicted of supplying information to the Germans on the movement of British shipping, and hanged for treason at Wandsworth Gaol.

In 1943 the 29th Division of the American Army arrived in the city, and the American Navy established a base in the Cattewater. They brought some of their customs and activities, introduced baseball to the area and formed their own local team, the Plymouth Yankees, which played on Saturday evenings at Pennycross Stadium, with gate receipts being given to local charities. In January 1944 the US Army opened a camp at Vicarage Road, St Budeaux, which housed forces making preparations for the D-Day landings.

By the middle of 1943, of the 12,000 children who had been evacuated, 8,000 had returned, but ninety schools had been destroyed or seriously damaged and many secondary schools had moved to other towns. Devonport High School for boys was evacuated to Penzance, Sutton Secondary School to St Austell, Devonport High School for Girls to Tiverton, Plymouth Girls' School to Newquay, and St Boniface College to Buckfast Abbey. Plymouth College stayed at Hyde Park Corner.

In November 1941 plans were announced for the first of three new villages for evacuees and war service staff to be opened, sponsored by the National Service Hostels Corporation on behalf of the Government. These would consist of brick-built accommodation blocks with kitchens, electric lighting, a sick bay and their own police stations. The first one had provision for 3,000 people, with families accommodated in rooms with four bunks in two tiers and single women in dormitories of twenty bunks. It included three large kitchens and eight 'feeding centres' that could seat up to 330 people at one sitting, looked after by a staff of eighty. Accommodation was free for the first two weeks but thereafter single residents had to pay 5s per week and families were charged double. A rest centre for 320 people was also to be erected on the outskirts of the city.

Bombing raids continued throughout 1943. In the early hours of 14 June there was a half-hour raid on the city centre and Plympton, during which over seventy high explosive bombs were dropped, but about half failed to detonate. One of the largest came through the roof at Greenbank Police Headquarters, bringing a large amount of masonry crashing down, and remained on the landing of the first floor outside the magistrate's court and over the prison cells and control room without exploding. The reserve headquarters at Widey Court were brought into use on a temporary basis until after the bomb was removed and the damage made good by the new National Fire Service and fire-fighters from Canada.

After a respite of about six months, the final aerial attack on Plymouth came on 30 April 1944, when an alert sounded at 3.15 a.m. Over thirty aircraft mounted an attack, their main target being the waterfront. Eighteen people were killed and seven were seriously injured in the Oreston area. At the depot of the Western National Omnibus Co. at Prince Rock, three firewatchers were killed and many buses were burnt out. An Anderson shelter was hit with the loss of six lives and a public shelter nearby was struck with a death toll of nine. Browning Road, Fisher Road and Beaumont Street at Milehouse, also suffered serious damage. Bombs landed on the Rising Sun public house, Crabtree, Laira railway sidings, the Tothill recreation ground and the Gas Co.'s recreation ground, leaving a huge crater but without causing any damage to vehicles nearby.

Three months later, audiences in the city were among the last to see a performance by one of the greatest of the wartime bandleaders. On 28 August Glenn Miller appeared at the Odeon Cinema, playing one of his final concerts prior to leaving for Europe where he was to plan a six-week tour. He boarded a flight for Paris on 15 December to supervise arrangements in advance, and the plane was lost over the English Channel.

During the war 1,172 Plymouth civilians were killed and 3,276 were injured. The city had the melancholy distinction of being the worst bombed city in Britain per capita in terms of civilian casualties. There had been 602 air-raid alerts and fifty-nine actual bombing attacks, while 3,754 houses were destroyed with a further 18,398 seriously damaged. Two Guildhalls, six hotels, eight cinemas, twenty-six schools, forty-one churches and a hundred public houses were among the buildings destroyed. The entire city centre had been obliterated except for St Andrew's Church, the Guildhall, the Regent Cinema (later demolished and replaced by Littlewoods store), and the offices of the *Western Morning News*. During the worst of the devastation the headmistress of a local girls' school posted a wooden sign saying *Resurgam* ('I shall rise again') over the door of St Andrew's Church, as a defiant emblem of the city's wartime spirit in the face of such adversity. On 23 May 1943 the first service since its destruction was held in the ruined church, and so many hundreds of people turned up to attend that police had to come and control the crowds. Ever since then the entrance of the building has been known as the *Resurgam* door, and a granite plaque with the word engraved is now permanently affixed above.

Meanwhile preparations for the invasion of Europe were being made, and the US Army was practising landings on the long stretch of Slapton Sands for the occasion, while the fleet was building up in the Sound. On D-Day, 6 June 1944, the V and VII

The Guildhall, on Royal Parade, survived the bombing raids of the Second World War. (Courtesy of M. Richards)

Corps of General Bradley's 1st Army, comprising some 36,000 troops, embarked from Plymouth for the Normandy landings. The first to leave were 110 ships carrying the men of the US VII Corps of the 4th Infantry Division, under the command of Rear-Admiral D.P. Moon aboard USS *Bayfield*. After joining up with more vessels and troops from Salcombe, Dartmouth and Brixham, they were among the first to land at Utah Beach. From 24 July the Vicarage Road camp was used as a receiving base for troops returning from France.

The Plymouth blackout was dropped in September 1944, and the Home Guard was ordered by the garrison commander, Colonel Thomson, to stand down in December. That same month, reduced lighting was once again permitted on some Plymouth streets, and an order that made the masking of headlamps on road vehicles compulsory was rescinded.

By spring 1945 the end of the war was clearly in sight. On 2 May the air-raid warning system was discontinued, Germany surrendered unconditionally on 7 May, and the next day was declared VE (Victory in Europe) Day. All street lights in Plymouth were switched back on on 11 May, for the first time in five and a half years. Life in the city slowly started getting back to normal, although there were no public feasts on a large scale because of food rationing, only street parties with neighbours clubbing together to give the children a treat as they laid tea tables out on the pavements. On 13 June public pleasure services started once again in the Hamoaze when the *Swift* sailed from Phoenix Wharf to the Royal Albert Bridge, and the *Lively* was put on as a relief boat. About 150 passengers made the journey. Celebratory bonfires were lit on Plymouth Hoe and at several other venues, while HMS *Renown* and other ships of the fleet provided a large firework display in the Sound. On 1 October the Great Western Railway began running the Royal Mail Postal special trains from Paddington to

Plymouth and Penzance, for the first time since September 1940. Two days earlier there had been a farewell to the old order with the running of the city's last tram, festooned for the occasion with bunting and Union Jacks, which started in the city centre and completed its final journey in the Milehouse depot. Since 1872 Plymouth trams had travelled an estimated 70 million miles and carried over 800 million passengers.

After the appointment in August 1945 of a decommissioning officer, the Vicarage Road United States' Army camp at St Budeaux was decommissioned a month later, and the remainder of the United States Naval Advanced Amphibious Base was closed.

Despite war-weariness Plymouth could look forward to peacetime with optimism, not least as a bold innovative plan had already been produced for the future of the city. In April 1944 the Plymouth City Council had held a special meeting to discuss the constitution of the new Reconstruction Committee, and the Plan for Plymouth was published. It was the joint work of James Paton Watson, the City Engineer, and professor Patrick Abercrombie of London University. The latter, who was already working on a reconstruction plan for Greater London, had been involved at the personal request of Lord Astor and the Emergency Committee, and was paid an £800 consultancy fee for his work. It was approved in principle by the council in August 1944. Lord Astor would have been a natural choice of chairman of the Reconstruction Committee set up to oversee implementation of the plan. However he had worked unremittingly throughout the war years as Lord Mayor, his health was not good, and he wanted to retire from public life. His term of office as mayor expired in November 1944, and he was succeeded by Alderman H.G. Mason, a Labour Member of the council.

Moreover he knew that the political tide was moving strongly towards Labour, locally as well as nationally. It was painfully evident to him and many others that

Union Street.

if his wife contested the seat again which she had held for over twenty-five years in the forthcoming General Election she would be heavily defeated, partly because of the general desire for a new beginning after years of Conservative-led National government, and partly as her maverick behaviour was making her a liability. Without consulting her, he advised the Sutton Constituency Party that she would not stand again for Parliament. Though she was initially angry with him, he was proved right when her successor as Conservative candidate lost in the election, held in July 1945. All three Plymouth seats returned Labour Members for the first time, with large swings and safe majorities. In Devonport the former minister Leslie-Hore-Belisha, standing again as a Liberal National, was rejected by voters in favour of Plymouth-born Michael Foot, whose father Isaac was a former Liberal Member of Parliament for Bodmin and was now the city's Lord Mayor. The Conservative backbencher Henry Guest was defeated in Sutton by Lucy Middleton, while in Drake the victorious candidate was Bert Medland, who had been Lord Mayor in 1935–6.

Even before the war, the city had urgently required major redevelopment. The shopping centre had expanded out of all proportion to its narrow streets, and the Civic Centre was too small to contain the number of administration staff needed. Slum clearance and re-housing schemes were barely keeping pace with the rapidly expanding population's needs, and an unchecked sprawl was threatening to erode parts of the surrounding countryside. War damage provided the city with the right opportunity to create something positive from the ashes, rather than piecemeal renovation. The plan foresaw what it called 'a great modern city', a place suitable for people to live and work in, respecting and safeguarding its links with the historic past while preparing for a prosperous future. It also argued that the centre of Plymouth was the commercial hub, and initial rebuilding work should be concentrated in that area. A deliberate intention was made not to reinstate what had been a large shopping centre in Devonport based on Fore Street, the primary reason being that the dockyard needed room to expand. Some of Devonport's prouder residents, particularly those who could still recall the old town's opposition to amalgamation in 1914, must have felt that this heralded a further erosion of its facilities and status.

Several activities associated with the city were identified in the plan. Plymouth needed to function as a naval dockyard, a naval and military centre, a shopping centre for a wide area, a light industrial centre, a port for sea and air, a fishing port and a residential area. According to contemporary employment statistics, 25 per cent of insured persons were associated with the Dockyard, 21 per cent with distributive trades, 17 per cent with building and public works, and 4 per cent with the hotel and boarding house industry.

A government committee headed by Mr Justice Uthwatt had recommended that legislation should be introduced permitting a local authority to declare war-damaged and obsolete areas 'Reconstruction Areas', with powers of acquisition at 1939 values. The Plan for Plymouth called for the area south and west of the Great Western Railway line from Weston Mill Creek to North Road Station, bounded by North Road, Clifton Place, Greenbank and Tothill Roads and then to the River Plym to be designated thus. Areas were to be set aside for industrial development in the Millbay-Stonehouse district between Union Street, West Hoe Road, Millbay Docks and the Royal Marine Barracks and also in the zone between Sutton Harbour and Prince Rock. This would merely be the first stage of an ambitious rebuilding scheme for the city which would amply fulfil the prediction and the vow *Resurgam*.

nine

Post-war Plymouth

The first step in inaugurating the Plan for Plymouth came in September 1945 when the city council approved the erection of temporary shops in Tavistock Road and Glanville Street, opposite the City Library, providing 22,000ft of space at a cost of £10,000, and similar shops in Princess Square, where 9,000ft would be provided at a cost of £4,500. Further approval for temporary shops was given by the council in 1946 for the erection of twenty-five temporary shops in George Street and Westwell Street, at a cost of £20,000, and it was decided to acquire 197 acres of the Derriford Estate.

Thanks to the use of prefabricated housing, good progress was made in the first few months of peacetime, and in November 1946 the 1,000th prefabricated house was occupied. Manpower to complete the reconstruction work was in very short supply, and once the city council wanted 100 men for a specific project, regardless of whether able-bodied or not. Fifty came forward, but thirty-eight had some excuse for not being able to work, leaving only twelve, and nine of these had left within a week. Only the use of prisoners of war helped to ensure that work was continued on building new houses and shops more or less on schedule.

A special service was held at St Andrew's Church on 21 March 1947 to commemorate the bombing of 1941, 'and to afford an opportunity to the council to dedicate itself to the task of the rebuilding of the city.' That same day the first kerbstone was laid in Raleigh Street, and the date engraved on it was regarded as commemorating the proper start of the reconstruction of Plymouth after the Second World War. Work had however already started early in the morning four days before, with the laying of a new drainpipe at Raleigh Lane. The gang's foreman was Gordon Harris, who was tragically killed in an accident in November while the old Westminster Bank in Bedford Street was being demolished. King George VI and Queen Elizabeth performed the formal opening ceremony of Royal Parade on 29 October when they came to inaugurate a tall flagstaff springing from a bronze cylinder in the shape of Drake's Drum, even though only the section from Westwell Street to Courtenay Street was finished.

To maintain the centre of Plymouth's reputation for quality shopping, the plan envisaged a series of precinct units, with a civic group based on St Andrew's Church, a rebuilt Guildhall and a shopping centre. A theatre group was planned for the Derry's Cross area, based on the Royal Cinema, with a new concert hall and theatre, eventually culminating in the long-delayed building of the Theatre Royal. Portland Square was to be the centre for educational and cultural facilities, in particular the siting and subsequent building of Plymouth Polytechnic, later the university. A West Hoe recreation precinct was suggested as the marine entrance to Plymouth, with a new

Royal Parade while under construction, 1946.

Royal Parade looking east, 1948.

Armada Way and Plymouth Sound, facing south.

conference centre and provision for amusement arcades, an open-air theatre, a stadium and a great rotunda. The station at the Great Western Passenger Dock was planned to bring visitors direct to this centre.

It was advised that any attempts to relieve congestion by merely widening the existing roads would be inadequate, and each unit in the new shopping centre was designed to try and discourage through traffic. The north-south axis, Armada Way, was planned as a route which would link the redesigned North Road station with the top of Plymouth Hoe, and present an uninterrupted 1,000-yard vista from the North Cross roundabout to the War Memorial on the Hoe. Abercrombie saw this as the plan's one great decorative feature, allowing visitors by train an immediate view of the Hoe, Plymouth's most famous landmark. The main east-west axis became Royal Parade, with a dual carriageway and a 75ft-wide central reservation laid out as a series of small gardens. This ambitious plan, it was emphasised at the start, would need to be sectionalised and carried out over a period of several years.

In March 1948 site allocations in Plymouth's new shopping centre were announced, and the remainder of Royal Parade was opened to traffic at the end of September. Dingles was one of the first to reveal its intentions with its ambitious plans for a four-storey department store, on Royal Parade. The five-storey Pearl Assurance House, also faced with Portland stone, would be built opposite using a complementary design which ensured that their corner features balanced each other. The rebuilding of Dingles and Woolworths began within a week of each other towards the end of 1949, Woolworths being the first department store to reopen for business in the city's reconstruction programme, twelve months later. Dingles – the first store in the south-west of England to include escalators – opened in September 1951, and recorded 40,000 visits from the public on the first day.

It had been estimated that about 2,200 tons per annum would be needed to complete the city's reconstruction. By February 1952, in view of increased demand

Plymouth Hoe, with Smeaton's Tower in the foreground and the War Memorial in the background. (© M. Richards)

for and decreasing imports of steel, there was a grave national shortage, and Plymouth Corporation was strongly advised to avoid using the metal in redesigning new buildings as far as possible. A target was launched for Plymouth to collect 450 tons, or 20lbs per household, equivalent to two iron pans and an old fireplace or a pair of bed-ends. The chairman of the Works Committee, Councillor W. A. Miller, launched a drive to collect as much scrap metal as possible. This would be picked up on normal refuse rounds, though extra vehicles would be employed. On 1 November it was announced that the scrap collection had yielded only 232 tons and the drive would therefore be extended for another week. Nevertheless the scheme was not as successful as everyone expected, and when it finished on 8 November 1952, only 280 tons had been collected.

Other hallmarks in rebuilding Plymouth were gradually achieved over the years. A new foundation stone was laid at St Andrew's Church in October 1949, and the rebuilt church was reconsecrated on 30 November 1957. Meanwhile in June 1955 it was agreed that the bombed-out shell of Charles Church, with its surviving walls left in situ, would be left as a memorial to the civilians who had lost their lives in the Second World War. Plans for rebuilding the railway station at North Road were announced in November 1951 and it was opened in March 1962. Bretonside bus station was opened in March 1958, and the new Plymouth Pannier Market eighteen months later.

In May 1954 Princess Margaret laid the stone marking the start of the reconstruction of the central library, the interior of which had been destroyed, and it was reopened in February 1956. Plymouth was fortunate in having appointed William Best Harris as city librarian. He was passionate about developing library services in the community with the provision of new branch libraries, lectures and children's events, as well as building up the book stock again. Having begun his career in his native Cardiff, he came to Plymouth as Senior Assistant Librarian in 1935, and was promoted to head of the service in 1947. He remained a tireless champion of the profession until his retirement in 1974, as well as a renowned local historian and broadcaster on local radio and television.

In 1949 the first part of the Whitleigh housing estate was occupied and the footbridge linking it with Honicknowle was opened. With its 362ft span, the longest of its kind in the country at the time, it was subjected to vigorous testing before being brought into use. In September 1951 it was announced that demolition of the Pembroke Street area of Devonport, the first major slum clearance scheme in England since the end of the war, would start in twelve months. Sir Thomas Sheepshanks, Permanent Secretary at the Ministry of Housing and Local Government, opened the 10,000th post-war municipal dwelling to be built by Plymouth City Council on 22 June 1954. Most of the building targets were met, and by November 1952 1,017 council houses and 138 dwellings provided by private developers had been built. By 1956 14,374 council houses and 2,283 private houses had been completed since the end of the Second World War, as well as eighteen primary and six secondary modern schools. The cost of land acquisition and clearance was £4.5 million, new roads, drains and sewers £432,000 and new buildings £6 million.

Demolition of old buildings sometimes caused controversy, occasionally of a light-hearted nature. At a public inquiry in 1953 into the Plan for Plymouth, held at the Devonport Guildhall, questions were asked about the need to demolish twenty-two public houses in Stonehouse. The town clerk, Mr Paton Watson, said he did not think the public houses were open when the men had their tea breaks; 'It is tea they drink nowadays.'

By 1955 most of Royal Parade and New George Street was completed. The Guildhall, rebuilt to designs created by the city architect, H.J.W. Stirling, was opened in September 1959 by Field-Marshal Lord Montgomery. In April 1962 Queen Elizabeth the Queen Mother opened the Tamar Bridge, and two months later the new Laira Bridge was opened by Lord Chesham. The Civic Centre was opened by Queen Elizabeth II in July 1962, thus bringing together under one roof various civic departments that had been scattered throughout the city since the destruction of the old Municipal Office building in Guildhall Square. When the new Law Courts were opened by Lord Denning in 1963 it marked the end of sixteen years of the official post-war reconstruction.

After the war, people gradually returned to the city which they had had to leave at short notice during the height of the Blitz, and before long the population not merely returned to its pre-war level but surpassed it. Just as urgent as the construction of the new city centre was the provision of new housing for the homeless. Nearly 20,000 houses, it was estimated, would be required in the ten years to 1955. This figure included the need to replace 6,833 houses destroyed in the Blitz, 6,277 slum or 'blighted' properties which needed replacement, plus about 1,000 more houses to take account of the pre-war shortage. Prefabricated buildings satisfied the short-term demand but new housing estates were needed to provide a lasting solution. In February 1952 it was announced that although 8,500 homes had been built since 1945 a further 10,000 were still needed. The cost of reconstruction work so far was announced on 10 March 1952 as £4.75 million.

Although not all ideas for residential development embodied in the plan were put into effect, some were incorporated in the new housing estates. The first of these was at Efford, followed by Ham, Honicknowle, Kings Tamerton, Ernesettle and Whitleigh, where estates were planned as self-contained entities with their own shopping centres, schools and recreational areas. The target of 20,000 houses was passed in 1964, some being private developments, and over 8,000 houses built by the Admiralty. Such development could only be achieved by spilling into the surrounding countryside, and Plymouth extended its boundaries further in 1951 to include Roborough and Tamerton, with the rapidly developing areas of Plympton and Plymstock following likewise in 1967. More council houses were built during the years at Southway, Eggbuckland, Leigham, Estover, Bellever and Chaddlewood.

Even after this, Plymouth continued to press for more boundary extensions. One proposal submitted to the Local Government Boundary Commission was for the annexation of Saltash and Torpoint on the other side of the Tamar. The 1971 Local Government White Paper proposed abolishing county boroughs which would have left the city with its population of 250,000 being administered from a council based at Exeter. Plymouth pressed unsuccessfully for the creation of a Tamarside county to include Plymouth, Torpoint, Saltash, and the rural hinterland, a proposal which was bitterly opposed by local authorities in Cornwall as well as those in Devon who preferred to keep the time-honoured geographical county boundaries intact. The city of Plymouth ceased to be a county borough on 1 April 1974 when responsibility for education, social services, highways and libraries was transferred to Devon County Council.

Twenty-four years later it became a unitary authority again under the recommendations of the Local Government Commission, chaired by John Banham. By this time the city of Plymouth was divided into twenty wards, seventeen of which elected three councillors and the other three elected two, comprising fifty-seven in all. In December 2003 the total electorate of Plymouth was 184,956. Members of the council stood for election as Members of national political parties, and local elections were held every four years. The council was headed by the Chairman and Vice-Chairman, Lord Mayor and Deputy Lord Mayor respectively, also comprising a Leader of the Council (the Chairman of the Cabinet) and a leader of each political group.

After 1945 the council worked hard to attract new industries to Plymouth, aiming to diversify industry as it was thought expedient to try and reduce the city's time-honoured and perhaps excessive dependence on the dockyard to provide employment. Among the first and most important new firms to arrive during peacetime were Tecalemit at Marsh Mills, Berkertex at Honicknowle and Rank at Ernesettle. Substantial land was made available for industrial estates on the edge of the city at Estover, Burrington and Southway, and several national and international companies were persuaded to set up new factories. This state of affairs was facilitated after Plymouth was designated a Development Area in 1958, a status rescinded in 1960 but partially restored when it became an Intermediate Development Area in 1969. By the middle of the next decade, many new industries had come to Plymouth, although paradoxically unemployment was still higher than the national average.

Everyone was prepared for the likelihood that in peacetime the naval presence at Devonport would diminish, and that employment in the dockyard would be reduced accordingly. Only six new ships were laid down in the post-war period, and the last of these, the Leander Class frigate HMS *Scylla*, launched in 1968, effectively marked the end of shipbuilding at the dockyard. The association of Devonport with the large aircraft carriers also finished when HMS *Ark Royal* was paid off in December 1978. The ship's anchor was presented to Plymouth by Admiral of the Fleet the Lord Hill-Norton on behalf of the Admiralty in April 1980, and is now to be seen at the Notte Street end of Armada Way.

In 1977 Dr David Owen, Member of Parliament for Devonport and Foreign Secretary, opened a new frigate complex in which three frigates could be dry docked completely under cover. The following year a new fleet maintenance base was opened by the Prime Minister, James Callaghan, and in 1980 Charles, Prince of Wales opened the new submarine refit complex. The Devonport workforce was fortunate to escape the drastic cuts which other naval dockyards faced in 1981, and several developments maintained it as a major British naval base.

The local tradition of hosting royal visits continued. Many have been the ceremonial events and military tours of inspection paid by royalty, particularly appropriate as Prince Philip, Duke of Edinburgh, was installed as Lord High Steward of Plymouth in 1960. Most notable were those by Queen Elizabeth II and the Duke of Edinburgh to present new Queen's and Regimental Colours to the Royal Marines in May 1969, scheduled to take place on the Hoe but moved to inside the Guildhall because of wet weather, and a walkabout by the Queen and the Duke in the city centre in August 1977 during the Silver Jubilee celebrations.

In 1950 the Drake constituency disappeared from the electoral map of Plymouth, but was restored in 1974 after another redrawing of the boundaries. The city had not seen the last of the Astor family, for in 1951 Lord and Lady Astor's youngest son John Jacob ('Jakie') regained Sutton for the Conservatives, representing the seat until he stood down in 1959. It remained in Conservative hands during two more general elections, until won by Dr Owen for Labour in 1966.

Born in Plympton, Owen was destined to become the city's best-known politician since Michael Foot. Having qualified in medicine, he spent eight years as Member for Sutton but after boundary changes he was elected for Devonport in 1974, narrowly defeating the popular backbench Conservative Member Dame Joan Vickers, who had held the seat since 1955. Foot said she was the only candidate he had ever known who personally canvassed every household in a constituency, and with her knowledge of defence policy as befitted someone representing a seat where naval issues were of paramount importance during her eighteen years at Westminster, she often performed better in Devonport than her party did nationally. Owen became a cabinet minister in 1977 and was at one time seen as a potential Labour leader, but he was increasingly opposed to the Labour party's leftward drift under the leadership of Foot in 1980, and in the following year he was one of the 'Gang of Four' who founded the new Social Democratic Party. A few years later it merged with the old Liberal Party to become the Liberal Democratic Party, a decision with which Owen disagreed. After the SDP was wound up he served the remainder of his last parliamentary term as an Independent Social Democrat before standing down from the House of Commons in 1992 and becoming a life peer, with the title Baron Owen of the City of Plymouth.

Next to Owen, Plymouth's most famous contemporary Member of Parliament was Alan Clark, son of art historian Kenneth Clark. Elected Conservative Member for Sutton in 1974, which he represented until standing down in 1992, he served in various junior ministerial posts at the Departments of Employment, Trade and Defence. He was long remembered for his outspoken, often unashamedly if not unfashionably right-wing views, and in his published diaries he made little secret of his distaste for Plymouth.

Although the post-war reconstruction was considered to have come to an end in 1963, new attractions opened and developments continued throughout the city over the years. Plymouth Zoo, in Central Park, adjacent to Home Park Football Ground, was opened in April 1962, and had 13,000 visitors during the first three days. Generally regarded as inferior to Paignton Zoo, only about thirty miles away, it closed in January 1978 after falling visitor numbers. Other features included a new shopping centre opened in November 1971 as a rebuilt and pedestrianised Drake's Circus, and a marina opened in 1973 at Ocean Quay. That same year ferries began running between Plymouth and France, and from 1978 they also went to Spain. The new Magistrates Courts were opened in 1979, the Armada Shopping Centre in 1988, and Plymouth Dome, a historically-themed visitor centre on the Hoe, in 1989.

The objective for the Barbican area, with its narrow streets and alleyways, adjacent to Sutton Harbour, had long been to rehabilitate the good buildings and to restore those of 'ancient lineage', where features had been defaced over time. Ironically, more of Plymouth's ancient buildings were destroyed or demolished in the 1950s by planners and developers than by enemy action during the Second World War. It was thanks to the efforts of the Barbican Association that many old Tudor buildings still remain largely unscathed to this day, and Plymouth thus still has the greatest single area of cobbled street surfaces in Britain.

In 1967 the Barbican district was only the second in England to be designated a Conservation Area. Over the next few years it became home to many art galleries and craft, design and antique shops, including the arcade The House That Jack Built, and the Barbican Centre. Among older attractions in the area were the Elizabethan House in New Street, a carefully restored captain's dwelling originally built around 1548,

Memorials to fishermen lost at sea adorn the RNLI store. (© Kim Van der Kiste)

containing the original windows and spiral staircase winding around an old ship's mast, with the restored Elizabethan Gardens a few yards away. Island House, a late-sixteenth-century building overlooking Sutton Harbour – which at various times had been a private home, a shop and an art gallery – became a Tourist Information Centre. Some of the Pilgrim Fathers were thought to have lodged there before their voyage to the new world in 1620, and a *Mayflower* passenger list was displayed on one side. The sea wall of West Pier, or Mayflower Pier, has been decorated with a large number of plaques commemorating the great voyages of colonisation that have started from Plymouth, as well as events such as the return of the Tolpuddle Martyrs to England from Australia in 1838 after their sentences were reduced, and on the wall of the RNLI store opposite are many memorials to fishermen lost at sea. Only a stone's throw away can be found Cap'n Jasper's, a snack bar overlooking the harbour. Originally established by 'the Captain', John Dudley in 1978 to help raise money for charity at the Barbican Regatta that year, it has become a permanent fixture, much loved by residents and tourists alike.

The new Plymouth Aquarium was opened on the Barbican in 1998. Nearby a large blue model fish dominates the end of Mayflower Pier. Nicknamed the 'Barbican Prawn', it is a striking example of the public art which has been used by the city council around the perimeters of the area to attract and direct tourists. Barely a corner of the area is not steeped in historical associations. Amongst the buildings overlooking Sutton Harbour is The China House, so named as Cookworthy reputedly stored his porcelain there, built around 1650 and thus Britain's oldest water's edge warehouse

Tolpuddle Martyrs landing stone. (© Kim Van der Kiste)

Cap'n Jasper's, the Barbican. (© M. Richards)

The Plymouth Aquarium. (© Kim Van der Kiste)

surviving in Britain. For some years it stood empty, but in 1992 it was leased by a brewery and converted into a pub and restaurant, with lofts, hoists, old fittings, casks and crates as part of the décor.

With pressure on all land within the city boundaries increasing year by year, constructive use had to be made of every area available, even to the extent of filling in some of the shallower areas of water. In 1972 the creek above Stonehouse Bridge, which ran past Millbridge to Pennycomequick and beyond to the bottom of Ford Park Cemetery, was reclaimed with some 600,000 tons of ballast and rubble. The result produced an extra nineteen acres of recreational land, the use of which was divided between playing fields, football pitches for local schools, and hardstanding for car boot sales.

The Falklands conflict against Argentina in the spring and early summer of 1982 saw a burst of renewed activity at the Royal William Yard, which worked a twenty-four-hour day at full stretch for several weeks in order to equip the Royal Navy and requisition civilian ships for the Fleet. When ships sailed for the South Atlantic Ocean on the beginning of their campaign in April, large crowds of Plymothians gathered at Devil's Point to wave them goodbye and wish them good luck. Civilian ships entered Plymouth Sound and went upstream to the dockyard to be refitted as warships. When the Fleet arrived home in July, the paths and cliffs were lined with crowds waving flags and holding up 'Welcome Home' banners. Each ship was escorted into the harbour by tugs, throwing up triumphal arches of water while helicopters flew overhead in salute.

The 'Barbican Prawn'. (© M. Richards)

From the mid-1980s onwards Plymouth's recent achievements were overshadowed by anxieties about the state of the dockyard, which had for several hundred years been the area's main employer. The British armed services were experiencing cutbacks, especially the Royal Navy, as emphasised by the recent closure of dockyards at Chatham and Portsmouth. Although Devonport yard survived, the new ships being built were fewer in number, and all were to a higher specification so they would need less refitting and maintenance. In 1947 the dockyard had a workforce of 21,000, but by 1981 this had fallen to 15,000. In 1987 the government leased the yard and all its facilities to a private company, Devonport Management Ltd. They had to tender for every naval job in competition with all other yards, at a time when other commercial shipyards in Britain were closing down for lack of work. Before long the new company had reduced the workforce by another 3,000. With the end of the Cold War in 1990, defences were slimmed down further still, and by 1992 the dockyard employed less than 5,000.

At the same time, the Ministry of Defence was relinquishing land which it had held for many years. In the 1950s Mount Batten became a main base for the Air and Sea Rescue service and their launches became a familiar post-war sight moored in the Cattewater. At the same time it was the headquarters of the Southern Maritime Air Region, which controlled the work of the squadrons based at RAF St Mawgan, Cornwall. The formal end of flying came on 5 March 1960, when a special ceremony was held at the base. Number 19 Group Coastal Command RAF left Mount Batten in 1968, which marked the beginning of the run-down of the station. The ceremony for the disbanding of the RAF Marine Branch was held at Mount Batten on 8 January 1986, and RAF Mount Batten closed on 5 July 1992, with the land and buildings being subsequently handed over to the Plymouth Development Corporation. Nevertheless the Royal Marines Commando Brigade remained in Plymouth, with an extended base for its logistic regiment at Marsh Mills, a new £2 million base for its assault craft section at Turnchapel Wharf, and a refurbished Citadel to give its artillery regiment modern accommodation.

The navy withdrew completely from the Royal William Yard in 1992, and seven years later the South West Regional Development Agency took over the yard. In partnership with regeneration developer Urban Splash, it made a major investment in transforming the old brewhouse and bakery into new apartments and working spaces. Commercial premises were designed with shops, restaurants and bars in mind.

The city remained largely free of the civil unrest which sporadically affected other urban centres of England during the 1980s. Nevertheless there were mass protests in the city centre in 1989 against the unpopular community charge or 'poll tax', led by the Anti-Poll Tax Federation. Less expected, and more shocking, was an arson attack on Dingle's flagship store in Royal Parade during the Christmas shopping season in December 1988 by animal rights protesters, angered by the store's selling of fur. Fire extensively damaged the upper floors, over a hundred firemen tackled the blaze, and damage estimated at over £13 million was caused.

The main theatre for Plymouth and surrounding area, the Theatre Royal, had been proposed in the 1943 Plan. Financial constraints delayed the commencement of building for over thirty years, and it opened rather belatedly in 1982. The main theatre had seating for 1,300 and the building included a smaller studio theatre, the Drum, for more experimental productions. Later, the Theatre Royal opened a production and education centre, TR2, on the reclaimed waterfront site at Cattedown.

Dingles, Royal Parade, after the arson attack of December 1988.

Such facilities were supplemented by the fringe Barbican Theatre. Many amateur dramatic societies and schools of dance in Plymouth performed regularly at the Athenaeum Theatre, Devonport Playhouse, and the Georgian Globe Theatre in the Royal Marine barracks.

During the beat boom of the 1960s, the city's main venue for popular live music acts was the ABC Cinema at Derry's Cross. The Beatles played there twice on tour at the height of Beatlemania, in November 1963 and October 1964, with two shows on each evening, while their rivals the Rolling Stones did likewise on a British tour in August 1964. In September 1967 The Beatles made a more informal public appearance on Plymouth Hoe, while taking a break from making their film *Magical Mystery Tour*. From the late 1960s onwards for several years the major music venue in the city for classical, pop and rock concerts was the Guildhall, where the progressive rock trio Emerson, Lake & Palmer played their first gig in August 1970, while the Van Dike Club in Exmouth Road and Woods Club in the city centre staged smaller shows. At the height of punk rock's popularity in August 1977 Woods hosted a date by the SPOTS (Sex Pistols On Tour Secretly) when the group were seeking anonymity in order to play live while evading the attention of local authorities trying to ban them because of their controversial reputation. Classical performances were also staged regularly at the Theatre Royal, while Plymouth Pavilions was opened in 1991 on the site formerly occupied by Millbay station. As the largest indoor venue in the area, it staged regular music events for all tastes from rock and pop to jazz, ballet, and other live events.

Home Park and the Hoe hosted large outdoor concerts, while the latter was also the venue for the BBC Radio 1 Roadshow one day each summer from 1973 until its final season in 1999. Plymouth made an ideal setting for regular events and festivals including the British Fireworks Championships and Music of the Night, a massive outdoor production held every two years in the Royal Citadel involving the efforts of the 29th Commando Regiment, Royal Artillery, the Royal Artillery Band, the band

ABC PLYMOUTH 63300

ON THE STAGE
FOR ONE NIGHT ONLY
THURSDAY, AUGUST 27th AT 6.15 & 8.30

THE

ROLLING STONES
MILLIE & THE 5 EMBERS
& ALL STAR COMPANY
STALLS & CIRCLE 12'6, 10'-, 7'6
Advance Booking Office opens July 27th

An advertisement for the Rolling Stones' appearance in Plymouth on their summer 1964 tour – the only occasion they played in the city.

of Her Majesty's Royal Marines, and hundreds of local amateur performers. Plymouth Music Accord, a marketing organisation for classical music, consisted of many amateur and professional orchestras and choirs such as the South West Sinfonietta, Plymouth Symphony Orchestra, the Philharmonic Choir, Opera South West, the City of Plymouth Concert Band, the Ten Tors Orchestra, the University of Plymouth Choir and Orchestra and Plymouth Jazz Club.

The city became the subject of a prestigious musical composition when the City Fathers commissioned the Plymouth-born composer, orchestrator and conductor Ron Goodwin to write the *Drake 400 Suite*, including six movements each depicting various facets of the area's seafaring traditions for the Drake 400 Commemorative Festival, celebrating the return of Drake to Plymouth after his round the world voyage. It received its first public performance in the Guildhall on 24 September 1980 with Goodwin conducting the Bournemouth Symphony Orchestra. Eight years later he was commissioned to write a similar piece, the *Armada 400 Suite*.

The Plymouth Arts Centre regularly offered visiting displays of work by local, British and international artists, with many independent art house and foreign films shown in the centre's own cinema, while there were smaller and privately owned galleries on the Barbican. Two artists who came to Plymouth and based themselves for many years in the Barbican became nationally famous in their own right. One was Beryl Cook, whose good-humoured pictures of flamboyant, buxom characters in everyday life were widely exhibited and published as limited edition prints and as greetings cards. The other was Robert Lenkiewicz, whose starkly realistic and often controversial portraits, particularly of what he called 'the hidden community', including the homeless and mentally ill, frequently polarised opinion of the day.

Since the music hall era of the late Victorian age, Union Street had been a centre of Plymouth's nightlife for over a century. After the First World War it was the main site for cinemas, and after the Second World War it was home to bars, discos and casinos. The Palace Theatre continued its tradition of attracting many top stars of stage and screen for many years, particularly after the old Theatre Royal closed in 1937. It is remembered especially as the venue where legendary film comedians Stan Laurel and Oliver Hardy made their last appearance onstage in May 1954 when both, particularly Hardy, were in failing health. With the increasing popularity of television its takings declined, and it underwent various changes of ownership and use, becoming a bingo hall and then a disco. For years Union Street had a notorious reputation for rowdyism after closing time, and as a red light district. Other clubs and bars were established at the Barbican Leisure Park, built on the old gasworks site at Coxside in 1998 and including a multiplex cinema, restaurants, bars, nightclubs and ten-pin bowling. At around the same time several bars opened on Mutley Plain and in the surrounding area, not far from the city's main student population.

Although Plymouth had no motorway links, the national network was within easy reach via the A38 dual-carriageway Devon Expressway to the M5 motorway which ended at Exeter. The A38 Parkway, which went east to west across the geographical centre of the city, was also readily accessible. Access as the 'gateway to Cornwall' was maintained by road via the Torpoint Ferry and the Tamar Bridge. From 1973 a regular international ferry service provided by Brittany Ferries operated from the site directly to Roscoff in Brittany and Santander in Spain. Early in the twenty-first century changes were planned that would see Plymouth revert from being mostly a naval port, where British and other foreign warships and submarines regularly docked, to being a regular destination for cruise liners, as was the situation before the Second World War.

By the 1970s there was a noticeable decline in the number of ships regularly using Sutton Harbour and the Cattewater. As commercial shipping decreased sharply, there was a corresponding increase in pleasure boating. Single-handed transatlantic races, the Fastnet races and various round-the-world events, organised by the Royal Western Yacht Club, were responsible for bringing more yachts to the inner basin at Millbay, while amateur yachtsmen made use of facilities in the new marinas at Sutton Harbour and Ocean Quay. Such sporting activities helped to perpetuate Plymouth's time-honoured seafaring traditions, as did one of Britain's most renowned yachtsmen of the modern age, Francis Chichester, a Devonian by birth. On 28 August 1966 he sailed from Plymouth on a single-handed circumnavigation of the globe, and was welcomed home by crowds from all over the country which gathered on Plymouth Hoe nine months to the day later, an achievement acknowledged by a knighthood the following month. However, Chichester fell ill whilst taking part in a single-handed transatlantic race in the summer of 1972 which he was unable to complete, had to be rescued, and died in the Royal Naval Hospital a few weeks later.

Air travel to and from Plymouth was based at Roborough, four miles north of the city centre, where the airport had been opened in 1931. By the beginning of the twenty-first century, the issue of redevelopment or relocation to provide and enable jet and other flights to continental Europe and beyond was a controversial one. Due to the airport's suburban location, further runway expansion was impossible and public opinion towards building a new airport to the east of the city was fiercely divided between anticipated economic benefits to local business and environmental concerns regarding speculative building on green field land. In 2007 Plymouth Airport operators revealed plans to sell much of the present airport land for residential and other purposes to raise cash to offset rising losses due to dwindling commercial activity. The need for a local airport was brought into question, particularly with the proximity of another at Exeter, about forty minutes away by road.

Plymouth railway station and Plymouth Citybus between them provided a strong network of local and national travel routes. Council licensing of hackney and private hire taxis increased, but suggestions that rush-hour congestion could be eased by reinstating the old tramway system or running light commuter trains along the old branch line routes to Tavistock, Turnchapel and Yealmpton met with little enthusiasm. The controversial proposal of a congestion charge option, adopted in London and other large cities, was ruled out by the main parties at council elections, though the issue seemed unlikely to go away.

For several centuries the economy of Plymouth was traditionally linked to its coastal location focusing around fishing and the military. The recent decline of these industries resulted in greater diversification towards a service-based economy based on healthcare, food and drink, and call centres, with electronics, advanced engineering and boat building still maintaining a prime role. By the end of the twentieth century, in terms of retail, Plymouth was ranked second in the South West and twenty-ninth nationally. As the largest regional city in Devon and Cornwall, it had a potential catchment area of over 720,000 people with an annual high street expenditure of over £600 million being spent in the city. An annual influx of an estimated 11.8 million tourists was another major contributor to the local economy.

In the education sector, Plymouth College of Technology was founded in 1965, later becoming a Polytechnic and in 1992 a university, the largest in south-west England and the fourth largest in the UK with over 30,000 students, almost 3,000 staff and an annual income of around £110 million. In October 2005, the *Sun* newspaper voted it as having the most bizarre degree course in the country, the BSc (Hons) in Surf Science and Technology, centred on surfing equipment design and business related to surfing. The College of Further Education, established in 1970 and renamed City College Plymouth in 2007, located on the site once occupied by Devonport station, was long established as one of the largest institutions of its kind in the country, with courses from the most basic to Foundation Degrees, and enrolling more than 20,000 students a year. The Plymouth College of Art and Design at Charles Cross offered courses relating to the world of art and design, while the University College of St Mark and St John, at Derriford, specialised in teacher training.

Sporting traditions were maintained by Plymouth Argyle Football Club, based at the Home Park stadium in Central Park, playing professional soccer in the English Football League's Championship division, with Plymouth United and Plymouth Albion Rugby Clubs playing their home games at the Brickfields. Adjacent to the new Brickfields rugby stadium was the Plymouth athletics track, while the annual Plymouth half marathon started and finished on the Hoe. Plymouth Cricket Club had teams and clubs at Plympton and Plymstock, and there was a golf club at Staddon Heights, with a nine-hole pitch and putt course in Central Park. International yacht racing was based around the Royal Western Yacht Club at Queen Anne Battery, while the Royal Plymouth Corinthian Yacht Club had a clubhouse on the Hoe and there were sailing clubs on the Rivers Plym, Tamar and Yealm.

Plymouth became the headquarters and regional television centre of BBC South West with studios in Mannamead, and a Carlton (ITV) television studio at Langage, as well as a new Plymouth city digital television station 'One Plymouth'. The BBC also had regional radio stations in Radio Devon and Radio Cornwall, and the city's main commercial radio station, Plymouth Sound, opened in 1975. In 1993 the *Western Morning News* moved from city centre premises in New George Street to new headquarters and printworks at a building at Derriford, designed in the shape of a ship by architect Nicholas Grimshaw.

Soon after the millennium Plymouth embarked on a new project of urban redevelopment. The 'Vision for Plymouth', launched in November 2003 by architect David Mackay, and backed by Plymouth City Council, envisaged regeneration on a scale second only to that of the post-war reconstruction period, embracing large areas of the city centre which were to be demolished, redesigned and completely rebuilt by 2020. Plymouth, it claimed, now had a new vision for the twenty-first century 'and the people of Plymouth are ready to adopt the "Mackay Vision" with energy and enthusiasm.' It took account of the 1990s when Plymouth was seen to be going through a period of decline. The city was said to be suffering a general lack of confidence, due to a decline in the defence sector, vulnerability in its manufacturing industry, low levels of entrepreneurship, high levels of unemployment, inability to attract private sector investment, low incomes and low skills, and areas of extreme disadvantage. In November 1998, unemployment in the inner city waterfront community of St Peter's Ward stood at 17.6 per cent, against 1.7 per cent in the comparatively affluent suburb of Plympton; and according to the 1998 Index of Deprivation which measured unemployment, ill-health and general living conditions, four wards in Plymouth were regarded as among the worst 10 per cent in England.

Against this background, an opportunity was seen for Plymouth to be recognised as a regional growth centre, and its 'potential to deliver accelerated growth as part of a quality agenda, in line with the Government's Sustainable Communities Plan; to reassert Plymouth's role as a regional centre; to challenge intra-regional disparities; to be part of the European Network of Cities to be a city that is confident about itself again.' It saw the vision of the public realm as being of the highest quality and a physical expression of the values of society, where every building formed part of the city and could contribute to the scale of enclosure. 'The street is a shared space and conflicting interests should be accepted as part of urban living.' For the city centre, it proposed that a greater intensification and density of mixed-use development should be introduced to include new residential, leisure and cultural evening uses, and improvements to the quality of the built environment and the public realm with improved links to the waterfront; taller buildings; shared attractive spaces; quality landmark buildings; and improved public transport interchanges.

For the cultural quarter, it envisaged an area dedicated largely if not wholly to cultural facilities and creative industries, which would eventually incorporate university, museum, library and other cultural activities. A recommendation was made that regeneration was extended to the east side of Sutton Harbour, being the main tourist area of Plymouth as well as a working harbour with a thriving fishing industry, and towards the Hoe with a mix of commercial and residential developments. More use could be made of the city waterfront, as the Hoe was Plymouth's promenade with spectacular views across Plymouth Sound, and long acknowledged as one of the most impressive natural harbours in the world. Other proposals included new and refurbished visitor attractions with piers and walkways along the foreshore, and water transport links from the Hoe to Sutton Harbour, Millbay and beyond. The Millbay Docks area presented particular opportunities for transformation, with proposals for a major mixed commercial and residential scheme, a new boulevard link to the city centre, a centre for marine science and research, a new cruise terminal, and commercial marine employment uses.

In conclusion, the new Vision for Plymouth looked forward enthusiastically to a future in which Plymouth could now aim to be the prime city for accelerated growth in the far south-west, with the potential to raise its population from 241,000 in 2003 to 300,000 by 2026; significantly reduce intra-regional disparities through targeted area action programmes; continue to invest in city growth strategy sectors to create new jobs; deliver 33,000 new dwellings by 2026, 4,200 affordable homes by 2016 and 17,000 new jobs through 220 hectares of new employment land; and deliver a radically different approach to transport in the city, whilst continuing investment in key road infrastructure projects linked to regeneration priorities.

The Drake Circus shopping centre opened in 1971, which was later found to have concrete cancer, and Charles Cross car park were both demolished in 2004. They were replaced by the £200 million Drake Circus shopping centre, which opened in

The Drake Circus shopping centre, behind Charles Church, 2007. (© Chris Downer)

The Eastlake Walk shopping precinct, shortly before demolition in 2004. (© Colin McCormick)

The Drake Circus shopping centre, opened in October 2006. (© Colin McCormick)

October 2006 and welcomed an estimated 60,000 visitors on its opening morning. The appearance of this futuristic-looking shopping centre behind the civilian war memorial at Charles Church provoked some controversy. Some thought its unsightly appearance did injustice to the dead of the Second World War, while its defenders claimed that its picturesque backdrop to the church created a striking combination of traditional and modern architecture. Nationally and locally, it soon attracted much adverse criticism, including an ironic architectural 'award' for being the single worst building in the United Kingdom. Following development of the new shopping centre, shop rents in the city centre were significantly increased, pushing smaller retail outlets out of the marketplace.

At the same time proposals were made that the Civic Centre municipal office building in Armada Way, dubbed by some local residents as an eyesore and 'the worst council building in Britain', should be demolished on the grounds that it was in a poor state of repair, and that changes in popular architectural taste and the council's need for finance should outweigh the historical architectural significance. Nevertheless, because of its quality and period features it was made a listed building by English Heritage, which called it 'one of the most important civic centre buildings of the 1950s in the country', and argued that in addition to its technical architectural merits, it was symbolic of the energy of Britain emerging after the devastation of the Second World War and showed the hope and aspirations of that newly confident Plymouth. The body, said a spokesman, believed that it was 'a building to be proud of, and a striking testimony to the spirit which guided the rebuilding of the city.'

Throughout its history, Plymouth has been a town (or one of three), later a city, in which the old has been able to co-exist peacefully, if sometimes a little uneasily, alongside the new. The Luftwaffe and the developers between them may have done their best to wreak havoc on the time-honoured fabric of bricks, mortar and design for various reasons, but spirited conservationists have always been prepared to defend Plymouth's heritage. One cannot but hope that the situation will remain broadly the same, and that tradition is accorded due respect notwithstanding the ever-present need, or at any rate desire, for change and progress.

Bibliography

Books

Bracken, C.W., *A History of Plymouth* (Plymouth; Underhill, 1931); n.e. Wakefield, SRP, 1970

Chalkley, Brian, Dunkerley, David and Gripaios, Peter (eds), *Plymouth, Maritime City in Transition* (Newton Abbot; David & Charles, 1991)

Clamp, A.L., *The story of Mount Batten, Plymouth* (Plymouth; PDS, nd, *c.* 1980)

Fleming, Guy, *A century of Plymouth: Events, People and Places over the 20th Century* (Stroud; Sutton, 2007)

———— *Plymouth: A Pictorial History* (Chichester; Phillimore, 1995)

Gerrard, John, *The Book of Plymouth* (Buckingham; Barracuda, 1982)

Gill, Crispin, *Plymouth: A New History* (Exeter; Devon Books, 1993)

———— *Plymouth Historians: Inaugural Presidential Lecture to the Old Plymouth Society upon its Reforming* (Plymouth; Old Plymouth Society, 1992)

———— *Sutton Harbour* (Tiverton; Halsgrove, 1997)

Goodall, Felicity, *Lost Devon: Devon's Lost Heritage* (Edinburgh; Birlinn, 2007)

Harris, Helen Joy, *Drake of Tavistock* (Exeter; Devon Books, 1988)

Hunt, Peter (ed.), *Devon's Age of Elegance: Described by the Diaries of the Reverend John Swete, Lady Paterson and Miss Mary Cornish* (Exeter; Devon Books, 1984)

Imrie, Robert, and Raco, Mike, *Urban Renaissance? New Labour, Community and Urban Policy* (Policy Press, 2003)

Jewitt, Llewellynn, *A History of Plymouth* (Plymouth; W.H. Luke, 1873)

Mais, S.P.B., *Glorious Devon* (London; Great Western Railway Co., 1928)

Oppenheim, M.M., *The Maritime History of Devon* (University of Exeter, 1968)

Robinson, Chris, *Plymouth Then & Now* (Plymouth; Pen & Ink, 2004)

———— *Victorian Plymouth: As Time Draws On* (Plymouth; Pen & Ink, 1991)

Scott, Reg, *Plymouth People: The Story of the Plymouth Guild of Community Service, 1907–1982* (Plymouth Guild of Community Service, 1982)

Stonehouse Residents Association, *A Stonehouse Century: Stonehouse Peninsula Remembered* (Plymouth; PDS, 2002)

Trewin, J.C., *Portrait of Plymouth* (London; Hale, 1973)

Twyford, H.P., *It Came to Our Door: The Story of Plymouth Throughout the Second World War* (Plymouth; Underhill, 1975)

Van der Kiste, John, *Royal Visits to Devon and Cornwall* (Tiverton; Halsgrove, 2002)

Walling, R.A.J., *The Story of Plymouth* (London; Westaway, 1950)

Wasley, Gerald, *Devon in the Great War, 1914–1918* (Tiverton; Devon Books, 2000)

———— *Devon in the 1930s – The Way We Were* (Tiverton; Halsgrove, 1998)

———— *Plymouth: A Shattered City* (Tiverton; Halsgrove, 2004)

Whitfeld, Henry, *Plymouth and Devonport in Times of War and Peace* (Plymouth; E. Chapple, 1900)

Woodward, F.W., *Citadel: A History of the Royal Citadel* (Plymouth, Exeter; Devon Books, 1987)

———— *Forts or Follies? A History of Plymouth's Palmerston Forts* (Tiverton; Halsgrove, 1997)

Worth, R.N., *History of Plymouth* (Plymouth; William Brendon, 1890)

Journals and Newspapers

Devon Life
The Times
Western Evening Herald
Western Morning News

Internet

Plymouth Data: The encyclopedia of Plymouth history, www.plymouthdata.info

A Vision for Plymouth, Plymouth City Council website, www.plymouth.gov.uk

Index